P9-CQZ-488

All-in-One
Sunday School

Volume 2

Winter

by Lois Keffer

Group

Loveland, Colorado
group.com

Dedication

To Christy, who shares her adventures in spiritual formation with me
as only a beloved daughter can.

Group resources really work!

This Group resource incorporates our R.E.A.L. approach to ministry. It reinforces a growing friendship
with Jesus, encourages long-term learning, and results in life transformation, because it's

Relational
Learner-to-learner interaction enhances learning and
builds Christian friendships.

Experiential
What learners experience through discussion and action
sticks with them up to 9 times longer than what they simply
hear or read.

Applicable
The aim of Christian education is to equip learners to be both
hearers and doers of God's Word.

Learner-based
Learners understand and retain more when the learning
process takes into consideration how they learn best.

All-in-One Sunday School

Volume 2
Copyright © 1992, 2011 Lois Keffer

Visit our website: **group.com**

All rights reserved. No part of this book may be reproduced in any manner whatsoever
without prior written permission from the publisher, except where noted in the text and in
the case of brief quotations embodied in critical articles and reviews. For information, visit
group.com/customer-support.

Unless otherwise indicated, all Scripture quotations are taken from the *Holy Bible,* New Living
Translation, copyright © 1996, 2004. Used by permission of Tyndale House Publishers, Inc.,
Carol Stream, Illinois 60188. All rights reserved.

Credits
Author: Lois Keffer
Cover Design: RoseAnne Sather
Interior Design: Jan Fonda and Suzi Jensen
Illustrations: Matt Wood

ISBN 978-0-7644-4945-1
Printed in the United States of America.
10 9 8 7 6   18 17 16 15 14

TABLE OF CONTENTS

THE LESSONS

INTRODUCTION

Dear friend in children's ministry,

As the world lights up for the coming of our Savior, all the delights of the season await you in Volume 2 of *All-in-One Sunday School!* You'll find thoughtful but lively Advent lessons that give kids a deeper appreciation for what Jesus' coming means to us. And in January we pick up stories from Jesus' life, helping kids grasp the enormity of love and power he embodies. Of course, there's a special lesson for Valentine's Day, and plenty of fascinating learning for the rest of your winter quarter!

Like you, I have always been drawn to kids, and they to me. They pick me out in grocery store lines, on busy sidewalks, and from passing cars. I think it's because they recognize someone who's never grown up! My teaching never became very "adult"—oh, no! Why? Because I saw the look of boredom that came over kids' faces when they sat down with the same ol' workbooks at Sunday school that they were used to year after year.

But when Sunday school involved active challenges, storytelling, and play, all melded into learning experiences with carefully crafted questions to help kids tie scriptural truth into their own lives—WOW! ZINGO! ZAP!—the learning lights went on! Discipline problems melted away. In our small church, grade school kids of all ages learned together.

Before we knew it, the adults wanted some of what the kids were getting, so we scheduled special intergenerational Sundays when the walls came down and the whole church learned together. And that's how *Sunday School Specials* was born, almost 20 years ago. At that time, we had no idea that one little book of lessons would turn into a series of four, or that the four would continue to find favor in the marketplace for years and years. Thank you to all who have faithfully bought these books! And praise God, who continues to surprise us!

So here's our new format: updated content, a fresh face, and a year-long scope and sequence to turn the four *Sunday School Specials* books into *All-in-One Sunday School*. Volume 1 begins with fall quarter; Volumes 2, 3, and 4 continue with winter, spring, and summer quarters respectively. So your favorite *Sunday School Specials* lessons, plus a few totally new and some updated ones, now form a through-the-year curriculum. Just so the adults don't feel left out, we've noted certain lessons that would be appropriate for intergenerational learning.

If you have a smaller Sunday school, are cramped for space or short on teachers, *All-in-One Sunday School* is just what you need to keep lively Bible learning going in your church without stretching your resources. Teachers can volunteer week by week, month by month, or in whatever pattern works best. Best of all, you can combine your grade-school kids and be assured that everyone will get the most out of each week's lesson to apply foundational Bible truths to their lives.

I'm so excited to make this resource available to you. I hope you'll love it as much as I've loved working on it!

Lois Keffer

ACTIVE LEARNING IN COMBINED CLASSES

Research shows people remember most of what they do but only a small percentage of what they hear—which means kids don't do their best learning sitting around a table talking! They need to be involved in lively activities that help bring home the truth of the lesson. Active learning involves teaching through experiences.

Children do things that help them understand important principles, messages, and ideas. Active learning is a discovery process that helps them internalize the truth as it unfolds. Kids don't sit and listen as a teacher tells them what to think and believe—they find out for themselves. Teachers also learn in the process!

Each active-learning experience is followed by questions that encourage kids to share their feelings about what just happened. Further discussion questions help kids interpret their feelings and decide how this truth affects their lives. The final part of each lesson challenges kids to decide what they'll do with what they've learned—how they'll apply it to their lives during the coming week.

How do kids feel about active learning? They love it! Sunday school becomes exciting, slightly unpredictable, and more relevant and life-changing than ever before. So put the table aside, gather your props, and prepare for some unique and memorable learning experiences!

Active learning works beautifully in combined classes. When the group is playing a game or acting out a Bible story, kids of all ages can participate on an equal level. You don't need to worry about reading levels and writing skills. Everyone gets a chance to make important contributions to class activities and discussions.

These simple classroom tips will help you get your combined class off to a smooth start:

♦ When kids form groups, aim for an equal balance of older and younger kids in each group. Encourage the older kids to act as coaches to help younger ones get in the swing of each activity.

♦ In "pair-share," everyone works with a partner. When it's time to report to the whole group, each person tells his or her partner's response. This simple technique teaches kids to listen and to cooperate with each other.

♦ If an activity calls for reading or writing, pair young non-readers with older kids who can lend their skills. Older kids enjoy the esteem-boost that comes with acting as a mentor, and younger kids appreciate getting special attention and broadening their skills.

♦ Don't worry too much about discussion going over the heads of younger children. They'll be stimulated by what they hear the older kids saying. You may be surprised to find some of the most insightful discussion literally coming "out of the mouths of babes."

♦ Make it a point to give everyone—not just those who are academically or athletically gifted—a chance to shine. Affirm kids for their cooperative attitudes when you see them working well together and encouraging each other.

♦ Keep in mind kids may give unexpected answers. That's okay. The answers given in parentheses after questions are simply suggestions of what kids *may* say, not the "right" answers. When kids give "wrong" answers, don't correct them. Say something like: "That's interesting. Let's look at it from another viewpoint." Then ask for ideas from other kids. If you correct their answers, most kids will soon stop offering them.

HOW TO GET STARTED WITH ALL-IN-ONE SUNDAY SCHOOL

Teaching Staff

When you combine Sunday school classes, teachers get a break! Teachers who would normally be teaching in your 4- to 12-year-old age groups may want to take turns. Or, ask teachers to sign up for the Sundays they'll be available to teach.

Lesson Choice

The lessons in the *All-in-One Sunday School* series are grouped by quarter—fall, winter, spring, and summer—but each lesson can also stand on its own. Several of the lessons contain suggestions for using an intergenerational approach, inviting parents and other adults in the congregation to join the class. You may want to schedule these lessons for special Sundays in your church calendar.

Preparation

Each week you'll need to gather the easy-to-find props in the You'll Need section and photocopy the reproducible handouts. Add to that a careful read of the lesson and Scripture passages, and you're ready to go!

QUICK-GRAB ACTIVITIES

What do you do when kids arrive 15 minutes early? When one group finishes before others do? When there's extra time after class is over? Get kids involved in a Quick-Grab Activity!

How I'm Feeling Faces Board

Use newsprint or a white board or chalk board for this activity. Write "How I'm Feeling Faces" across the top. As kids arrive, invite them to draw a face that shows how they're feeling—happy, sad, mad, rushed, sick, upset or lonely. The first time you use this activity, explain it to the kids and brainstorm different emotions they might express on the board. Ask them to initial the faces they draw.

Encourage kids to ask questions about each other's feelings. For instance, if someone draws a sad face, a friend might say, "I'm sorry to see you drew a sad face. Did you have a bad day at school?"

This can be a great tool for kids to use to learn to care for each other in deeper, more meaningful ways. You may also want to use it during guided prayer times with the children.

By the way, don't forget to draw your own "How I'm Feeling Face." Your participation will encourage the kids to participate as well. And if they discover that you've had a rough day, you'll be surprised at how extra thoughtful they will be!

Best or Worst Thing This Week Board

You guessed it—this works just the like the How I'm Feeling Faces Board. In fact, you may want to alternate the two. Invite kids to draw or write about their best or worst experiences of the week. This board may start off with superficial experiences, but it will soon grow to a depth that surprises you.

Kids really want to tell about themselves—to know and be known. One drawback of filling every minute of Sunday school is losing that intimate moment when a child would like to talk about a concern or unburden herself of a fear. A medium such as this lets kids form a pattern of sharing themselves in a nonthreatening way, which can lead to the sense of true community we all seek within God's family.

Prep and Takedown

If kids love your class—and they will!—they'll be more than willing to do everything that needs to be done to get going. So if you need chairs, handouts or supplies arranged, task your charming youngsters with the job. Have you noticed how a child's sense of worth soars when it is his particular responsibility to see that each person has a handout? Or when she gets to pack the teacher's bag?

Small jobs like these also create ownership in the class, which translates to less discipline issues. *Hey this is my class so I'm not going to mess it up!*

Whenever you say during class, "I need a helper, " you'll get a wind-farm's worth of waving arms. The same goes for before and after class as well! So put all that youthful enthusiasm to work and you'll have kids champing at the bit before class even begins.

Jabber Mat®

Group's Jabber Mat® is an on-the-floor, all-out-fun resource loaded with games and challenges for your class. Once you've used it, you'll wonder what you ever did without it! Purchase this instant go-to activity mat from Group Publishing (group.com/jabbermat).

LESSON AIM

To help kids see that ★ through faith in Jesus they are a light to all nations.

OBJECTIVES

Kids will

✓ play a game of Battle of the Blowers,

✓ review the history of Israel,

✓ discover their role in God's promise to be blessing to all nations, and

✓ create an apple candleholder to celebrate sharing God's light.

YOU'LL NEED

❏ masking tape
❏ pingpong ball
❏ battery-lit candle
❏ Bible
❏ red apples*
❏ sturdy plastic knives
❏ sprigs of pine (fresh or artificial)
❏ pencils
❏ taper candles
❏ lighter
❏ photocopies of the "Pine-Apple Candleholder" handout (p. 17)

Always check for allergies before serving snacks.

BIBLE BASIS

Psalm 118

Israel was a tiny nation at the crossroads of territory contested by international superpowers. After the heydays of David and

Solomon, Israel became a pawn, tossed for centuries between the Babylonians, Persians, Egyptians, Greeks, and finally the Romans. Some conquerors let them keep their national identity and worship God in the ways set down in the Torah, the five books of Moses. Others, to spread their particular culture, worked to wipe out Judaism, burning all known copies of the Torah, executing priests and desecrating the Temple. During this era, many Jews lost the ability to speak and read Hebrew.

God's people, who conquered Canaan under Joshua and began such a hopeful journey, ended up being swept about on the stormy seas of international politics. Yet, they never forgot God's promise that a king from the line of David would rule in Jerusalem forever. Psalm 118 recalls God's goodness in the past and prophesies his goodness in the future with a triumphant king returning to Jerusalem amidst the waving of boughs and cries of "blessed is he who comes in the name of the Lord."

The sheer number of Psalms that point to the coming of Christ is amazing. We begin the season of Advent with Israel's troubled history, their hope in God's faithfulness, and foreshadowing of a coming king, the likes of whom history had never seen.

1 Peter 2:9

When God began his relationship with Abraham and called him out of Ur into an unknown land, it was to establish a special people, a holy people who would be a light to all the nations. The Torah, the five books of Moses, lay out how they were to live. After that, the books of Judges, Kings, and Chronicles tell their struggles, their coming together under earthly kings, and peril from empires without and idol worship within. The prophets write of longing to return to the homeland after Jerusalem's destruction.

The life, death, and resurrection of Jesus let all who believe in him gain full and free adoption into this honored family. We who believe are now the light carriers. What an honor. What a joy!

UNDERSTANDING YOUR KIDS

With this lesson we turn from Thanksgiving to Advent. We've been celebrating God's amazing gifts to us while, in truth, kids have been eyeing what they'll put on their Christmas lists!

During this season it's a challenge to get kids to focus on God, whose glorious abundance of gifts to us culminates with the unmatchable gift of his Son. The parade of Christmas programs and parties easily overshadows the true marvel of the season: that God's faithfulness to us began at Creation, continues throughout the seasons of planting and harvest, and takes on the whole new aspect of God with us as we look forward to the coming of our Savior. Use this lesson to help kids realize this truth!

The Lesson ☺

Battle of the Blowers

Lay two masking tape lines about one and a half yards apart. Each line should be long enough to accommodate half the kids.

Say: **Today we're going to begin with the Battle of the Blowers. Everybody puff out your cheeks for me so I can see that you're nice and full of air.**

Puff out your own cheeks to show them what you mean and to get a good laugh from the kids.

Say: **Good job! I'm going to choose three championship blowers to stand on this masking tape line.** Choose any three kids to stand on one line. **The rest of you, please stand on the opposite line.**

Place a pingpong ball between the two lines.

Say: **This game is very simple. The goal is to blow the ball across the other team's line. You can blow from your knees or your bellies, whichever position you think will give you the best advantage.**

If kids begin to complain that the team of three is at a great disadvantage, ignore them, or remind them that there are championship blowers on that team.

Say: **No one blow until I say "blow."** Allow kids to position themselves; then pause a few moments to build the tension. **Ready…set…blow!**

When the team with more kids wins quickly, say: **Let's have a rematch! I'm sure our championship blowers will win this time.**

Repeat this two or three times. Then sit down with the kids and act puzzled.

Say: **I don't get it. We had some great championship blowers over here, but they couldn't seem to win. I must've set up the game wrong. Maybe I should have put the lines further apart.**

Let the kids respond.

Say: **Okay, here's what we'll do.**

Choose three kids from the larger team to stay where they are. Send the rest of the team over to join the three championship blowers. Play the game once more and give a big cheer when the championship blowers finally win. Then join the kids on the floor.

Say: **Strangely enough, this game reminds me a lot of today's Bible story. You see, the nation of Israel was a very** small nation. But there were huge kingdoms all around it. It was kind of like our team of three against everyone else. First one empire would conquer Israel, then another, and then another. They were just too small to stand against any of the world powers of ancient times. But they never gave up. They had a secret hope. And I'm going to let you in on that secret hope in just a minute.

Collect the pingpong ball and gather the kids in a large story circle.

BIBLE STUDY

A Light to All Nations (Psalm 118; 1 Peter 2:9)

Gather kids in a circle. Say: **It's important to know a little history of Israel so we can understand the promises God made to his people and be ready for Jesus' coming.**

It all started when God called Abraham to go to a new land. I need someone to be Abraham. Have "Abraham" sit in the center of the circle. **Abraham had a wife named Sarah. Who will be Sarah?** Have "Sarah" join "Abraham." **After many long years they had a son named Isaac.** Have an "Isaac" sit in the center.

Now this might seem like a small start for a nation, but listen to this promise God made to Abraham. God told Abraham to look up and count the stars in the sky. There are way too many stars in the sky to count, aren't there?

Say: **God promised that someday his family would be larger than all the stars! There was another, even more important promise God made to Abraham: God said, "Through your family, all the nations of the world will be blessed." That's the secret hope I was talking about earlier. Whatever happens in our story, I want you to remember that secret hope!**

Then Isaac grew up and had twins named Jacob and Esau. Invite two more kids to the center of the circle. **And so Abraham's family grew and grew until it was a whole nation, the nation of Israel, just as God promised.**

But other nations were much, much larger. There were nations that were so huge they swallowed up other nations. Like Egypt, for instance. It was bigger than many, many Israels put together. At one time, because of a drought, everyone from Abraham's family lived in Egypt. They became slaves. Life was hard.

Have the kids in the outer circle stand, stomp around the "Israelites" in the center of the circle once, and sit back down.

Say: **God set the Israelites free from the Egyptians. Eventually he helped them conquer and build the land of Israel**

Teacher Tip

You might play a CD of soft, instrumental music as kids draw. Soothing background music increases kids' ability to concentrate during quiet, thoughtful activities such as this one.

that looks something like the Israel we know today. There were times when Israel loved God and worshipped him and shined a light to all the nations, just as God planned.

Give the Israelite group a battery-lit candle.

The book of Psalms records the songs the Israelites sang to God. I'm going to read part of one. It has a part for a reader and a part for a group to answer. You'll be the answering group. Here's your part: His love continues forever.

Have the kids repeat the response until you're sure they have it.

Say: Now I'm going to read from Psalm 118. Each time I pause, you answer by saying, "His love continues forever." Let kids practice. Everyone please stand in honor to God as we perform a version of this psalm together.

Thank the Lord because he is good;
   His love continues forever.
Let the people of Israel say:
   "His love continues forever."
Let the family of Aaron say:
   "His love continues forever."
Let those who respect the Lord say:
   "His love continues forever."

Thank you; you may sit down.

Then the great kingdom of Assyria rose in the east. Their armies threatened Israel. But Israel still hoped in God. Have the Israelites in the middle hold up their candle while the outside circle stomps around them one time and then sits down.

The Egyptians threatened Israel and made them pay heavy taxes. Once again, have the Israelites in the middle hold up their candle; have those in the outside circle stomp around the Israelites one time and then sit down.

Next, the Babylonians came and destroyed the Temple and the city of Jerusalem. They took many Israelites captive. Repeat the same process as above.

Say: Now all of you can sit together in the middle. Throughout history the same thing happened over and over. After the Babylonians came the Persians, then the Greeks, and finally at the time of Jesus' birth, the Romans. But the Israelites always remembered their secret hope that they would be a blessing to all the nations.

Signal one of the inner circle of Israelites to stand up and hold the candle.

Listen to some other parts of Psalm 118 that tell this part of Israel's story. I hope you remember your line, because that's how the Psalm ends.

14

I will not die, but live,
   and I will tell what the Lord has done.
The Lord has taught me a hard lesson,
   but he did not let me die.
God bless the one who comes in the name of the Lord.
   We bless all of you from the Temple of the Lord.
The Lord is God, and he has shown kindness to us.
   With branches in your hands, join the feast.
   Come to the corners of the altar.
Thank the Lord because he is good…
   His love continues forever.

Say: **Through everything that happened, God's people knew that he was with them and that they would be a light to all the nations. ★ Our faith in Jesus means we are a light to all nations, too. And now I have a great surprise for you!**

LIFE APPLICATION

Pine-Apple Candleholders

Have kids form groups of four. On a table set out large red apples, sturdy plastic knives, pencils, sprigs of fresh or artificial pine, candles, and copies of the "Pine-Apple Candleholder" handout.

Say: **Choose one carrier from your group to bring an apple for each person, one to bring pencils and handouts, one to bring sprigs of pine, and one to bring candles and knives.**

Say: **If you look at the Bible verse on your handout, you'll find the surprise I promised you.**

Ask someone to read aloud 1 Peter 2:9. Then ask:

♦ **Who is the "you" in this verse?** (God's people; the Israelites; I'm not sure.)

Say: **That's the surprise. The "you" in this verse is you! All of you sitting here with me in this room. All of us who believe in Jesus! You see, Jesus came to Earth to invite everyone to be part of God's family. When we put our faith in Jesus, God adopts us into his ancient family and we become the carriers of God's light. ★ Our faith in Jesus means we are a light to all nations. Isn't that awesome?** Ask:

♦ **Why do you think we decorate our homes during Christmas?** (Because we are the light; because Jesus is the light; because it's pretty.)

♦ **How can we be the light of Jesus ourselves?** (We can do good things; we can act like Jesus.)

Say: **During the Christmas season we decorate our homes with lights to celebrate the fact that Jesus is coming. As believers in Jesus, we carry his light in our hearts, too. As a**

Teacher Tip

So there isn't a scramble for supplies, call out the items one at a time and have the carriers bring them back to their groups.

Teacher Tip

You may want to precut holes in the tops of the apples to hold the candles securely.

symbol of the light of hope that Jesus brings to the world, let's make these beautiful candleholders.

Demonstrate how to use a pencil to poke holes near the top of an apple, large enough to accommodate a sprig of pine. Tell kids how many pine sprigs they can use for their decorations. When all the pine sprigs are in place, have kids carefully cut a hole for the candle in the top of the apple with a sturdy plastic knife. If the candle doesn't fit tightly, wrap the bottom with a bit of plastic wrap.

Say: **Candles must always be used with your parents' permission.**

COMMITMENT

Shine God's Light

When Jesus came to Earth, he opened the way for everyone to become a part of God's family. Before, that was a privilege that belonged to the people of Israel. Now it belongs to all of us who put our faith in Jesus. ★ You who believe in Jesus are a light to all the nations!

♦ **What do you think about being part of God's special family?**

♦ **What does it mean to shine God's light?** (That we show others that we trust him; that we tell others about Jesus.)

♦ **How does Jesus' light shine in our lives?** (When we do loving things; when we give thanks to God.)

♦ **When you show your candle decoration to your family, what will you tell them about what you learned today?**

CLOSING

Help Us to Shine

Have kids gather around a table. Place a candle decoration in the center of the table and light it. Ask the kids to join you in prayer.

Dear God, thank you for the beautiful season of lights that's ahead of us. Thank you for including us in your family so that ★ we can be a light to all the nations of the world. Help us to shine with your love this week. In Jesus' name, amen.

Have kids take their candle decorations and their "Pine-Apple Candleholder" handouts.

PINE-APPLE CANDLEHOLDER

But you are a chosen people, royal priests, a holy nation, a people for God's own possession. You were chosen to tell about the wonderful acts of God, who called you out of darkness into his wonderful light. —1 Peter 2:9, NCV

Make a living candleholder with a shiny red apple as the base.

♦ Cut a hole around the stem of the apple about 1 inch deep and large enough to hold the base of a taper candle.

♦ Use a pencil to poke holes around the top of the apple. Push a sprig of pine into each hole. (The juice from the apple will keep the pine fresh for several days.)

♦ Carefully push the candle into its hole. If the hole is a bit too large, wrap the base of the candle with plastic wrap.

♦ Enjoy!

Caution: Be careful not to let the candle burn low enough to catch the pine on fire.

Permission to photocopy this handout granted for local church use. Copyright © Lois Keffer.
Published in *All-in-One Sunday School Volume 2* by Group Publishing, Inc., 1515 Cascade Ave., Loveland, CO 80538.

LESSON

LESSON AIM

To help kids understand that ★ Jesus is the Savior God promised.

OBJECTIVES

Kids or families will

✓ play a game to learn why they need a savior,
✓ participate in an interactive Christmas story,
✓ create Christmas projects that remind them that Jesus is the Savior God promised, and
✓ commit to telling others that Jesus is the Savior.

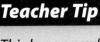

This lesson works well with an intergenerational class. You may wish to invite whole families to join you for this session.

YOU'LL NEED

❏ treats on a festive tray*
❏ Bibles
❏ photocopy of "God's Long-Ago Clues" handout (p. 29)
❏ materials for the learning centers of your choice:
❏ photocopies on green paper of the "Advent Holly Wreath" patterns (pp. 27-28)
  ❏ scissors
  ❏ red glitter glue
❏ photocopies of the "Christmas Votive-Candle Holder" instructions (p. 30)
  ❏ clean tin cans filled with ice
  ❏ pencils
  ❏ hammers
  ❏ nails
  ❏ newspapers
❏ photocopies of the "Baby-in-a-Manger Treats" instructions (p. 31)
  ❏ a mixing bowl
  ❏ a container of melted margarine*
  ❏ measuring cups
  ❏ peanut butter*

all-in-one
SUNDAY
SCHOOL

- ❑ marshmallow creme*
- ❑ chow mein noodles*
- ❑ a tablespoon measure
- ❑ large spoons
- ❑ small paper plates
- ❑ small pretzel sticks*
- ❑ orange circus peanut candies*
- ❑ fruit leather*

Always check for allergies before serving snacks.

BIBLE BASIS

Luke 2:1-20

It's always a joy to come back to Christmas! No matter how many times we revisit the story, our hearts are filled with the wonder and joy of that miraculous birth. The wonder lies in the great paradoxes that we can only begin to comprehend. The voice that once spoke our world into being confines itself to the coos and cries of a newborn. The hand that would some-day be pierced for us now clings fiercely to a young mother. Simple shepherds who expected nothing more than a long night with their sheep on a chilly hillside now answer an angelic summons to look in the face of deity. The Lord who possesses all the riches of heaven empties himself to enter a humble family. Men renowned for their wisdom travel a great distance to pay homage to a wordless infant whose wisdom is infinitely greater than theirs.

It's surprising, this plan of salvation that God set in motion 2,000 years ago. It's so unlike how we would have done it, so unscientific, so downright off-the-wall! Brilliant minds of the secular world rebel at the audacious simplicity of God's plan—to send a holy child who would live a perfect life, die a sacrificial death, and then rise to conquer Satan's power and offer eternal life to those whose faith is bold enough to believe him.

The joy is in the sweet realization that it's all true—that this infant Savior was born for you!

Isaiah 7:14; 9:6-7; 43:25; Jeremiah 23:5; Micah 5:2

For hundreds of years before Jesus' birth, prophets had been seeing God-given visions of his kingdom that was to come. The details of his birth and life and death are irrefutably written in Old Testament Scripture. Anyone who truly desires to investigate and compare prophecy to fulfillment can see and believe.

Schoolchildren learn to deal in cold, hard facts. They learn to observe and apply the scientific method—to create and test theories and hypotheses and determine if an experiment will bring the same results twice. Faith may be dismissed as superstition and old wives' tales. Or it may be accepted—there are many brilliant scientists and physicists who are so awed by the wonder of the universe they study that faith in an infinitely wise, powerful God is the only logical response.

It feels really terrific to point to Old Testament Scriptures that foretell with pinpoint accuracy important details of Jesus' birth, life, death, and resurrection. Your kids can direct skeptics of any age to these Scriptures and say, "You want proof? *Here's proof!*" Use this lesson to help kids see that Old Testament prophecies help us understand that baby Jesus truly is the Savior God promised.

☺ The Lesson

ATTENTION GRABBER

No Perfect People

Bring delicious-looking treats to class on a festive Christmas plate or tray. Place the treats where they'll be sure to be noticed as everyone arrives. If kids ask when they'll be allowed to eat the treats, tell them they'll find out in a few minutes.

Hold up the plate of treats and say: **Several of you have noticed these treats. They do look good, don't they? And I'd just love to share them with you. But you're going to have to qualify for them. You see, these are such perfectly wonderful treats that I can share them only with perfect people.**

Please line up facing me with the smallest person in front and the tallest person in back.

When everyone has lined up, approach the first child and ask:
♦ **Have you ever done anything you shouldn't do?**

When that child answers, "yes," say: **I'm sorry, I guess I can't give you a treat. You'll have to go sit down.** Ask the rest of the kids in line any combination of these questions.
♦ **Have you ever said anything you shouldn't say?**
♦ **Have you ever disobeyed a parent?**
♦ **Have you ever hurt someone's feelings?**
♦ **Have you ever gotten angry when you shouldn't have?**

One by one, dismiss everyone in line. When you're left holding the treats, say: **You know what? I've done all of those things, too. I guess I can't have any of these treats either.**

Set the plate of treats down and go sit with the others. Don't give any indication of what's going to happen next until kids grow restless and start to question you. Then say: **Well, I'm not sure what to do. My instructions were that I could share those treats only with perfect people. But none of us is perfect. We've all blown it sometime in our lives.**

Set the plate of treats aside.

Say: **I guess we'll just have to leave these treats until we can figure out what to do. I'm not giving up hope, though. People who believe in God never give up hope.**

Let kids offer suggestions until someone mentions that's why Jesus came. If no one offers that suggestion, bring it up yourself. Say: **No one is perfect. That's why God sent Jesus into the world. Do you remember the story of Creation?** Ask:
♦ **Who were the very first people God made?** (Adam and Eve.)
♦ **What did they do wrong?** (They ate fruit from the tree God had said not to eat from.)

> **Teacher Tip**
>
> If you happen to have a child who insists he or she actually is perfect, avoid getting into an argument with this gentle response: "It's great that you work at pleasing God. But God knew none of us could ever be perfect. So he sent his perfect son Jesus to be with us."

21

Say: **Adam and Eve sinned and disobeyed God. And ever since, every person who has lived has sinned and disobeyed God.** Hold up the plate of treats. **God has something wonderful to share with us—much more wonderful than these treats! It's called heaven.** Ask:

♦ **How would you describe heaven?** (Jesus is there; the streets are made of gold; we'll live there forever; we'll be very happy there.)

♦ **But there's no sin in heaven. So if we've all sinned, how do you think we can go there?** (We need Jesus to forgive our sins.)

Say: **God knew that people could never be perfect. So long ago, he promised to send a Savior who would take away their sins. God's prophets began writing about Jesus hundreds of years before he was born. Let's read some of the things they wrote.**

Have volunteers look up and read Isaiah 7:14; 9:6-7.

Say: **The prophet Isaiah wrote those words about Jesus, the Savior God would send into the world hundreds of years later. Listen to something else Isaiah wrote: "Comfort, comfort, my people, says your God. Speak tenderly to Jerusalem. Tell her that her sad days are gone and her sins are pardoned"** (Isaiah 40:1-2a)**.**

Distribute the treats as you say: **You're not perfect, and I'm not perfect. So God sent a Savior to pay for our sins.** ★ **Jesus is the Savior God promised. Because Jesus came, God can share heaven with us someday. Let's celebrate the story of his birth in a fun and different way.**

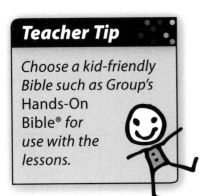

Teacher Tip

Choose a kid-friendly Bible such as Group's Hands-On Bible® for use with the lessons.

BIBLE STUDY

God's Clues (Isaiah 7:14; 9:6-7; 43:25; Jeremiah 23:5; Micah 5:2)

Before class, make a photocopy of the "God's Long-Ago Clues" handout, and cut apart the clues.

Say: **God's prophets planted clues throughout the Old Testament telling us what would happen when the Savior came. Raise your hand if you like solving mysteries. Good—I do, too! I have some long-ago clues that God's prophets wrote in the Old Testament that tell things that would happen when the savior of the world was born. I'm going to hide them and you're going to find them, but first I need you to form pairs. It's a good idea to have a reader and a prereader in each pair.**

After kids form pairs, have them sit with their partners facing one wall of your teaching area.

Say: **It's your job to make sure your partner doesn't peek** as I plant the clues behind you. So you can't hear me, please whistle "Jingle Bells" as loudly as you can. Are you ready? Start whistling!

As the kids whistle, hide the clues from the "God's Long-Ago Clues" handout.

Say: **To hunt for the clues, you need to link elbows with your partner. Any pair that lets go of elbows is out of the hunt. When all of the clues are found, join me here for the rest of the story. Ready? Go hunting!**

When kids rejoin you in the story area, congratulate them on their hunting efforts. Then say: **I'll call in your clues one by one. Who has Clue 1?**

Have one of the partners who found Clue 1 read Micah 5:2 aloud. It is reprinted here for your convenience.

"But you, O Bethlehem Ephrathah,
are only a small village among the people of Judah.
Yet a ruler of Israel will come from you,
one whose origins are from the distant past."

Micah 5:2

Ask:

♦ **What clue about the Savior's birth did you hear?** (That he would be born in Bethlehem.)

Say: **Excellent mystery solving! Now for Clue 2.**

"The Lord himself will give you a sign: The virgin will be pregnant.
She will have a son, and she will name him Immanuel."

Isaiah 7:14 , NIV

Ask:

♦ **What clue about our Savior's birth did you hear from that?** (That his mother would be the virgin Mary.)

Say: **That's right! Jesus' mother, Mary, wasn't yet married to Joseph. Jesus' father was God himself. Now let's listen to Clue 3.**

"For a child is born to us, a son is given to us.
The government will rest on his shoulders.
And he will be called: Wonderful Counselor, Mighty God, Everlasting Father, Prince of Peace.
His government and its peace will never end.
He will rule with fairness and justice from the throne of his ancestor David for all eternity. "

Isaiah 9:6-7a

Ask:

♦ **This is a little bit trickier. First, who knows what an "ancestor" is?** (Call on a volunteer.)

♦ **What clue did you hear about an ancestor of the Savior?** (That he would be related to King David.)

Say: **This is such an important clue! The Old Testament prophets say over and over that the Savior will reign on the throne of King David. Guess what! Jesus was born into the same family as King David, many, many generations later. Isn't that cool? Now I'll give you a big hint: The last clue is pretty similar. So who has Clue 4?**

" 'The time is coming,' says the Lord, 'when I will raise up a righteous descendant from King David's line.

'He will be a king who rules with wisdom. He will do what is just and right throughout the land.' "

Jeremiah 23:5

Ask:

♦ **What was the similar clue?** (That he would be born into David's family.)

Say: **Good sleuthing everyone! Now here comes the big important question.** Ask:

♦ **Who do these clues remind you of?** (Jesus!)

Exactly! There are many more clues in the Old Testament about how our Savior would come and what he would be like and what he would do. Today I just wanted to find the ones that talk specifically about Jesus' birth because we're going to celebrate that day pretty soon.

There's one more clue about the Savior that I want to share with you. Listen very, very carefully.

"I, I am the One who erases all your sins, for my sake; I will not remember your sins."

Isaiah 43:25, NIV

Ask:

♦ **What does this tell us about our Savior, Jesus?** (That he will take away our sins.)

Say: **That's right. ★ Jesus is the Savior God promised. We celebrate his birth because God promised from long ago that he would send a Savior to be born of a virgin, born in Bethlehem, born from the family of David to rule on David's throne to take away our sins! That's quite a gift, my friends.**

Let's hold up our hands, palms up. Please pray with me.

Pray: **Dear Jesus, you are the greatest gift of all time. We love you. Thank you. Amen.**

When Jesus takes away our sins, he makes us perfect

inside. Another Scripture in Isaiah says that he blows away our sins like a big cloud that disappears into the air. Let's all say "Poof!" like we're making a big cloud blow away! Ahhh... isn't it wonderful? Let's create something to help us celebrate that Jesus is the Savior God promised.

Before class, make a sample Advent holly wreath from the patterns on pages 27-28 (if this is one of the centers you've chosen to offer). Hold up the Advent wreath and say: **In just a few moments we'll be doing some Christmas projects. One of the choices is an Advent wreath like this one. Each section of the wreath has two Scripture passages printed on it. One is from an Old Testament prophecy—or "clue"—about Jesus' birth. The second passage is from the New Testament. It tells how that prophecy came true.**

Set the wreath aside and continue: **Seeing all the prophecy that came true at Jesus' birth helps us believe that ★ Jesus is the Savior God promised. When we study the rest of Jesus' life, we find even more connection with prophecies from the Old Testament.**

Let's get started on our projects!

Teacher Tip

It's a good idea to prepare a sample of each of the projects to show to the kids. You may want to recruit a teenage or adult helper to make the samples and help out during class.

LIFE APPLICATION

Christmas Learning Centers

Choose one, two, or all three of these Christmas learning-center ideas. Each is easy to prepare and fun for kids as well as adults. And each center allows kids to actively explore the important truth that ★ Jesus is the Savior God promised.

If you have time, let kids do all the projects. If time is limited, offer photocopies of the instructions from each center for kids to take home.

♦ **Advent Holly Wreath**—Photocopy the "Advent Holly Wreath" patterns onto green paper. You'll need one set of patterns for each person who chooses this project. Set out the patterns, scissors, and red glitter glue. Kids will cut out the four sections of the pattern and add red glitter glue to the holly berries. Then they'll attach the four sections to form a ring. This craft complements the Christmas Votive-Candle Holder below that can be placed in the center of the wreath as the Christ candle.

♦ **Christmas Votive-Candle Holder**—Before class, clean several small tin cans, and remove the labels. Fill the cans with water, and freeze them. Keep them frozen until class time by storing them in the church freezer or in a cooler. Set out pencils, hammers, nails, newspapers, the ice-filled cans, and a copy of the "Christmas Votive-Candle Holder" instructions. Kids will hammer cross designs into the cans, remove the ice, and insert votive candles.

♦ **Baby-in-a-Manger Treats**—Set out photocopies of the "Baby-in-a-Manger Treats" instructions, small paper plates, small pretzel logs, marshmallow creme, flavored cream cheese spread, chow mein noodles, a container of melted margarine, measuring cups, a tablespoon measure, a mixing bowl, and a large spoon. You'll also need orange circus peanut candies and a package of rolled fruit leather such as Fruit Roll-Ups. Kids will stir together a delicious "hay" mixture and put it on a plate; then they'll press pretzels into the hay to form a manger. They'll place a circus peanut "baby" on top after wrapping it with fruit leather to represent swaddling clothes. One recipe will make enough of the hay mixture for about 10 kids.

Announce when there are five minutes of working time left, then two minutes, then one. When you call time, have participants gather their projects and sit in a circle. Tell kids to place their crafts on the floor behind them.

COMMITMENT

Share the Savior

Say: **I'd like you to think for a moment about someone who doesn't know that ★ Jesus is the Savior God promised.**

Pause as kids think. Then say: **Now talk with someone sitting near you about a way you might tell that person about the importance of Jesus' birth. Tell your partner how you could share the good news about Jesus with that person.**

After partners have talked, ask volunteers to share their plans for telling someone about Jesus.

CLOSING

Christmas Thanks

Have kids hold their projects as you close with a prayer similar to this one: **Dear Jesus, thank you for coming to earth to be our Savior. Thank you for the joy that this special season brings to us because your coming means that we can look forward to being with you in heaven someday. Please help us tell others that ★ you are the Savior God promised. In your name we pray, amen.**

ADVENT HOLLY WREATH 1

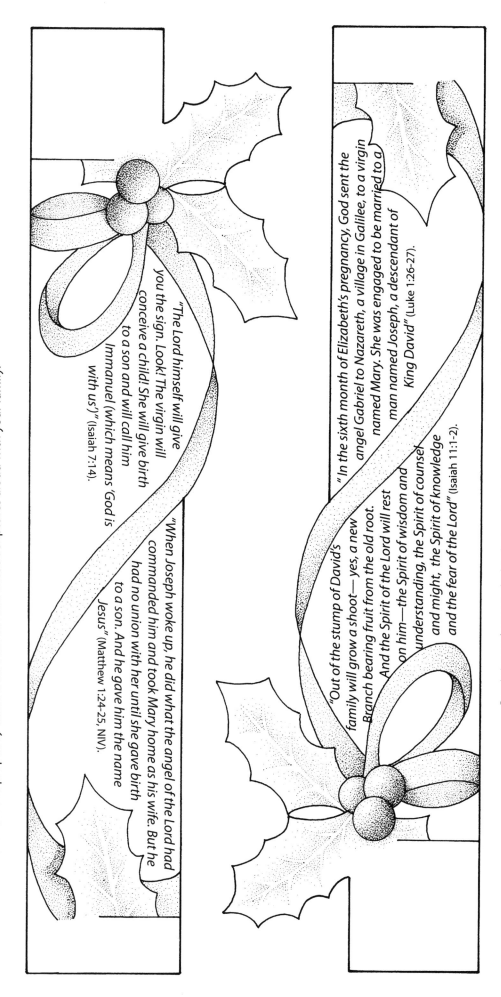

Cut around the outside of both sections; then cut the two slits in each section. Fasten these two sections together at the slits; then add the two sections from "Advent Holly Wreath 2" to form a circle. If you wish, add red glitter glue to the holly berries. At home, place a candle in a holder in the center of the wreath.

The first Scripture passage in each section gives an Old Testament prophecy about Jesus' birth; the second passage is from the New Testament and tells how the prophecy came true. Plan to read these Scriptures aloud with your family.

"The Lord himself will give you the sign. Look! The virgin will conceive a child! She will give birth to a son and will call him Immanuel (which means 'God is with us')" (Isaiah 7:14).

"When Joseph woke up, he did what the angel of the Lord had commanded him and took Mary home as his wife. But he had no union with her until she gave birth to a son. And he gave him the name Jesus" (Matthew 1:24-25, NIV).

"In the sixth month of Elizabeth's pregnancy, God sent the angel Gabriel to Nazareth, a village in Galilee, to a virgin named Mary. She was engaged to be married to a man named Joseph, a descendant of King David" (Luke 1:26-27).

"Out of the stump of David's family will grow a shoot— yes, a new Branch bearing fruit from the old root. And the Spirit of the Lord will rest on him—the Spirit of wisdom and understanding, the Spirit of counsel and might, the Spirit of knowledge and the fear of the Lord" (Isaiah 11:1-2).

Permission to photocopy this handout granted for local church use. Copyright © Lois Keffer.
Published in *All-in-One Sunday School Volume 2* by Group Publishing, Inc., 1515 Cascade Ave., Loveland, CO 80538.

ADVENT HOLLY WREATH 2

Cut around the outside of both sections; then cut the two slits in each section. Fasten these two sections together at the slits; then add the two sections from "Advent Holly Wreath 2" to form a circle. If you wish, add red glitter glue to the holly berries. At home, place a candle in a holder in the center of the wreath.

The first Scripture passage in each section gives an Old Testament prophecy about Jesus' birth; the second passage is from the New Testament and tells how the prophecy came true. Plan to read these Scriptures aloud with your family.

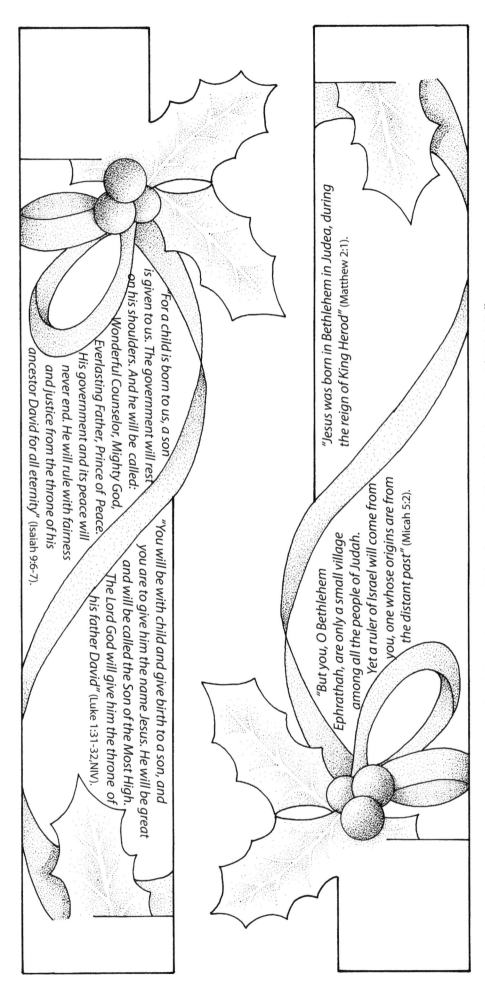

"For a child is born to us, a son is given to us. The government will rest on his shoulders. And he will be called: Wonderful Counselor, Mighty God, Everlasting Father, Prince of Peace. His government and its peace will never end. He will rule with fairness and justice from the throne of his ancestor David for all eternity" (Isaiah 9:6-7).

"You will be with child and give birth to a son, and you are to give him the name Jesus. He will be great and will be called the Son of the Most High. The Lord God will give him the throne of his father David" (Luke 1:31-32, NIV).

"Jesus was born in Bethlehem in Judea, during the reign of King Herod" (Matthew 2:1).

"But you, O Bethlehem Ephrathah, are only a small village among all the people of Judah. Yet a ruler of Israel will come from you, one whose origins are from the distant past" (Micah 5:2).

Permission to photocopy this handout granted for local church use. Copyright © Lois Keffer.

Published in *All-in-One Sunday School Volume 2* by Group Publishing, Inc., 1515 Cascade Ave., Loveland, CO 80538.

GOD'S LONG-AGO CLUES

  CLUE 1

"But you, O Bethlehem Ephrathah, are only a small village among all the people of Judah.

Yet a ruler of Israel will come from you, one whose origins are from the distant past."

Micah 5:2

 CLUE 2

"The Lord himself will give you a sign: The virgin will be pregnant. She will have a son, and she will name him Immanuel."

Isaiah 7:14, NIV

 CLUE 3

"A child is born to us, a son is given to us.

The government will rest on his shoulders.

And he will be called: Wonderful Counselor, Mighty God, Everlasting Father, Prince of Peace.

His government and its peace will never end. He will rule with fairness and justice from the throne of his ancestor David for all eternity."

Isaiah 9:6-7a

 CLUE 4

" 'The time is coming,' says the Lord, 'when I will raise up a righteous descendant from King David's line.

'He will be a king who will rule with wisdom. He will do what is just and right throughout the land.' "

Jeremiah 23:5

Permission to photocopy this handout granted for local church use. Copyright © Lois Keffer.
Published in *All-in-One Sunday School Volume 2* by Group Publishing, Inc., 1515 Cascade Ave., Loveland, CO 80538.

CHRISTMAS VOTIVE-CANDLE HOLDER

1. Use pencil dots to mark cross patterns on both sides of the ice-filled tin can. Make the dots about a half-inch apart.

2. Find a partner. Have your partner hold the can with several thicknesses of newspaper.

3. Use a hammer and nail to gently punch a hole through each dot in your pattern. Tap very lightly with the hammer. It does not take much force to punch through the can.

4. Hold the can upside down under warm water until the ice falls out.

5. At home, place a votive candle in your can. The light from the candle will shine through the holes and make the crosses glow!

Permission to photocopy this handout granted for local church use. Copyright © Lois Keffer.
Published in *All-in-One Sunday School Volume 2* by Group Publishing, Inc., 1515 Cascade Ave., Loveland, CO 80538.

BABY-IN-A-MANGER TREATS

1. Work together with other kids to make the following recipe for "hay."

   In a mixing bowl, blend:

   2 tablespoons melted margarine

   ¼ cup peanut butter

   Stir in 3 cups chow mein noodles.

2. Place a mound of hay on the center of a small paper plate.

3. Take twelve small pretzel sticks. Build them log-cabin style around the mound of hay; then press the hay against the pretzels to help them hold together. Now you have a manger!

4. Tear a piece of fruit leather. Wrap it around a circus peanut candy as you would wrap a blanket around a baby.

5. Place the circus peanut candy in the center of the manger to represent baby Jesus.

Permission to photocopy this handout granted for local church use. Copyright © Lois Keffer.
Published in *All-in-One Sunday School Volume 2* by Group Publishing, Inc., 1515 Cascade Ave., Loveland, CO 80538.

LESSON

3

LESSON AIM

To help kids understand that ★ Jesus' birth means God is with us.

Teacher Tip

This lesson works well with an intergenerational class. You may wish to invite whole families to join you for this session.

OBJECTIVES

Kids or families will

✓ experience having someone guide them,
✓ participate in an interactive story about the birth of Christ,
✓ learn about Christmas symbols and create a banner, and
✓ commit to being aware of God's presence in their lives.

YOU'LL NEED

❏ masking tape or garlands
❏ Christmas decorations
❏ candy canes*
❏ blindfolds
❏ a photocopy of the "One Special Night" story (pp. 36-37)
❏ scissors
❏ photocopies of the "Symbols of Christmas" handouts (pp. 39-42)
❏ various colors of construction paper or felt
❏ glue or glue sticks
❏ dowels (optional)
❏ Christmas music
Always check for allergies before serving snacks.

BIBLE BASIS

Matthew 1:18-25

Immanuel. First spoken by Isaiah in his Messianic prophecy, "Immanuel" is one of Scripture's most profoundly beautiful words. It means, simply, "God with us." Since the beginning of

all-in-one
SUNDAY
SCHOOL

the world, God has desired to be with us. Genesis 3:8-9 says, "When the cool evening breezes were blowing, the man and his wife heard the Lord God walking about in the garden. So they hid from the Lord God among the trees. Then the Lord God called to the man, "Where are you?'" Sin had disrupted their fellowship. God gave the Law to define sin and point the way toward holiness. But only the incarnation of God's own Son could make it possible for God to truly be with us.

Jesus walked on earth to show us who God is. Jesus died to redeem us from our sins. Jesus rose again to conquer death and give us eternal life. Jesus sent the Holy Spirit to guide and empower us. Immanuel, God with us. What a gift!

Luke 2:11-12

The angel gave the shepherds a sign to recognize the Christ child: He would be wrapped in cloths and lying in a manger. We can be a sign to fellow Christians and to the world that the Christ of Christmas is with us today!

UNDERSTANDING YOUR KIDS

Kids in today's society learn to be on their own at an early age. They rehearse important "home alone" rules with their parents. By first grade many kids know how to be safe as they walk home from school, how to use the house key to let themselves in, how to fix themselves a snack, and how to call Mom or Dad to report that they're safe at home. Can you see how the concept that "God is with us" is an important one for these kids?

There's so much to be excited about at Christmas. But the very best news you can give your kids is that God is truly with them, whether they're home alone, on a crowded school bus, confronting a neighborhood bully, or feeling secure with Mom and Dad close by. God's presence is the best of all presents!

ATTENTION GRABBER

Christmas Lane

Set up an obstacle course with Christmas decorations. Use garlands or masking tape to mark edges of a path about 3 feet wide and 15 feet long. Strew candy canes along the path.

Set up an obstacle course with Christmas decorations. Use garlands or masking tape to mark edges of a path about 3 feet wide and 15 feet long. Strew candy canes along the path.

Pair up participants as they arrive, matching older kids or adults with younger kids. Have pairs decide which partner will be the walker and which will be the guide. Blindfold all the walkers.

Say: **Walkers, your job is to walk down Christmas Lane without stepping on any candy canes. Guides, your job is to talk your partner through the lane. You may not touch your partner—just walk alongside and tell him or her where to step.**

After the first walker is a few feet into the path, have the next walker begin. When each pair finishes the path, greet the partners with applause and remove the walker's blindfold. If you have plenty of time, you may want to let the walkers and guides switch roles. When everyone has finished, gather the group and ask:

♦ **What was it like to walk through Christmas Lane blindfolded?** (Scary; exciting.)

♦ **Walkers, how did you feel about your guides?** (I trusted her; I hoped he would tell me the right thing.)

♦ **What would've happened if you hadn't had a guide?** (I might've tripped or broken something; I wouldn't have been able to stay on the path.)

♦ **Guides, how did you feel about your walkers?** (I wanted to take good care of him; I tried really hard to tell her where to step.)

♦ **How is what the guides did like what God does for his followers?** (God tells us how to live; God's words keep us on the right path.)

♦ **When the prophet Isaiah foretold Jesus' birth, he said Jesus would be called "Immanuel." Can anyone tell me what "Immanuel" means?** (God with us.)

♦ **Why would Jesus be called that?** (Because he is God, and he came to earth to be with people; because he is the way to God.)

Say: ★ **Jesus' birth means God is with us. Today we're going to celebrate that fact and discover through symbols of Christmas what it means to have God with us.**

Teacher Tip

It's best not to place any breakable ornaments in the path. For extra fun, play lively Christmas music as partners work their way through the path.

BIBLE STUDY

One Special Night (Matthew 2:1-11; Luke 2:8-20)

Say: **Let's review the Christmas story in a brand-new way.**

Before class, photocopy the "One Special Night" story. Cut apart the 15 verses and distribute them as evenly as possible among the partners.

Say: **Decide which partner will be the reader and which partner will lead the motions. I'll give you a couple of minutes to go over your verses together.**

Have the pairs stand in a circle in the order their verse or verses fall in the story. Explain that everyone should do the motions with the pair that's performing.

Introduce the story by saying: **And now, welcome to our presentation of the Christmas story, "One Special Night."**

Lead everyone in a round of applause as the story ends. Then say: **If you could be anyone in the Christmas story, I wonder who you'd chose to be. Turn and tell your partner who you'd want to be and why.**

Allow a few moments for partners to talk; then ask volunteers to share what their partners said.

LIFE APPLICATION

Symbols of Christmas

Say: **There are so many wonderful things about the Christmas story! We look forward to hearing it year after year. There are also lots of wonderful Christmas symbols and traditions we enjoy. Let's have some fun learning more about them.**

Distribute photocopies of the "Symbols of Christmas" handouts.

Choose volunteers to read aloud the explanation and Bible verse on or near each symbol. Then distribute scissors and have participants cut out the symbols.

Have partners or families use the symbols to create Christmas banners from construction paper or felt.

Decide whether you'll have each family make a banner or if you'll have each participant make his or her own banner. Even if individuals make their own banners, it's helpful to have them work in pairs so they can share ideas and work out problems together. Be sure that younger kids are paired with older kids or adult helpers.

Kids or families will need 11x17-inch rectangles of felt or construction paper for their banners. Have them fold the rectangles in half vertically and cut a pointed bottom four inches deep

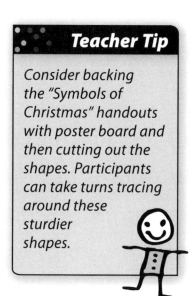

Teacher Tip

Consider backing the "Symbols of Christmas" handouts with poster board and then cutting out the shapes. Participants can take turns tracing around these sturdier shapes.

ONE SPECIAL NIGHT

(from Matthew 2:1-11; Luke 2:8-20)

1 In faraway Bethlehem one special night,
   tired shepherds watched over their sheep.
   (Rest cheek on hands.)
   Then the sky was suddenly filled with light,
   and the shepherds awoke from their sleep.
   (Sit up and look startled.)

2 "Good news I bring you," the bright angel said,
   "news that will fill you with joy:
   In Bethlehem-town, in a dark cattle shed,
   is born a brand-new baby boy."
   (Pretend to hold a baby.)

3 "This child is the Christ, the Savior of all.
   He'll be in a warm manger bed
   (pretend to pull up a blanket),
   wrapped in soft clothes, this baby so small,
   with straw to pillow his head."

4 Then suddenly angels filled the whole sky
   (make star bursts with fingers),
   singing God's glory and praise.
   "Peace upon earth," came their song from on high.
   The shepherds stood watching, amazed.

5 Then, in a twinkling, the angels were gone.
   (Cross hands; then pull them apart.)
   The night grew cold and still.
   But the shepherds remembered the heavenly song
   as they stood on their lonely hill.

6 "Let's hurry to Bethlehem," one shepherd said
   (pump arms as though you're running),
   "to find the holy child."
   And, sure enough, there in a manger bed
   lay Jesus, sweet and mild.

7 The little sheep's "baa" and the doves' soft "coo"
   were the baby's lullaby.
   The shepherds fell down and worshipped, too,
   (bow and fold hands),
   as a bright star shone in the sky.

8 "The Son of God has been born tonight!"
   (Cup hands around mouth.)
   The shepherds spread the word.
   And those who came to see the sight
   (clap hands to cheeks)
   could hardly believe what they heard.

9 Three wise men in a land far away
    saw the beautiful star.
    (Point upward.)
    "It tells of a special child born today,"
    they said. "We must travel far."

10 "God has sent us this special light
    to guide us on our way.
    (Point into the distance.)
    We'll cross the desert during the night
    and rest in the heat of the day."

11 So by-and-by, the wise men found
    Jesus and Joseph and Mary.
    Then the three wise men bowed to the ground
    and said, "Take these gifts that we carry."
    (Hold up cupped hands.)

12 Gold and sweet perfume they gave
    and thought, "Our gifts are small.
    For Jesus came the world to save
    (spread arms wide);
    he brings God's love to all."
    (Cross hands over heart.)

13 On Christmas Eve, some people still search
    for Mary's baby Son.
    But he's not in a manger and not in a church.
    (Shake head.)
    He lives in everyone.
    (Point both hands to heart.)

14 So when you see a star twinkling bright
    (make a star burst with fingers),
    in a crisp, quiet winter sky,
    remember the gift God gave that night
    and the angels that sang on high.

15 There's a gift that you can give Jesus, too.
    It's not too hard to find.
    To each person you see the whole year through
    (pretend to point to several people),
    be loving and gentle and kind.
    (Give a hug.)

Permission to photocopy this handout granted for local church use. Copyright © Lois Keffer.
Published in *All-in-One Sunday School Volume 2* by Group Publishing, Inc.,
1515 Cascade Ave., Loveland, CO 80538.

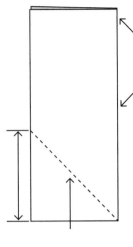

as shown in the margin illustration. Provide red, green, white, blue, yellow, gold, and brown construction paper or felt. Participants can trace around the symbol pattterns on their chosen colors, cut out the symbols, and then glue them in place on their banners.

If you choose to make felt banners, you may also want to supply slender dowels for hanging.

Play Christmas music as participants work on their banners. Encourage people who finish first to help others complete their banners.

COMMITMENT

Procession of Banners

When all the banners are complete, have everyone help clean up the work area and then line up for a procession of banners. Encourage everyone to sing "O Come, All Ye Faithful" as you lead the procession around the room or around the church building.

Close the procession by having everyone sit in a circle. One by one, invite participants to stand and explain why they chose to use certain symbols and what their banners mean to them.

When everyone has shared, say: **Our banners can be reminders that ★ Jesus' birth means God is with us. You may want to hang your banner in a window or on your front door. Or perhaps you'd like to give it away to someone who would enjoy its message.**

Have participants turn to partners and tell what they plan to do with their banners.

CLOSING

Christmas Greeting

Say: **Let's close our class with a special greeting.** Ask:
♦ **What special greeting do Christians use on Easter?** (Christ is risen; he is risen indeed.)

Say: **Let's make up a similar greeting for the Christmas season. You'll step up to someone, shake his or her hand, and say, "Jesus is born." The other person will respond, "God is with us." Let's try that together: Jesus is born; God is with us.**

Allow participants to exchange greetings with several people. Then close with a prayer similar to this one: **Dear Lord, what a difference it makes in our lives that you were born as a tiny baby long ago. Thank you for being with us. We love you. Amen.**

SYMBOLS OF CHRISTMAS

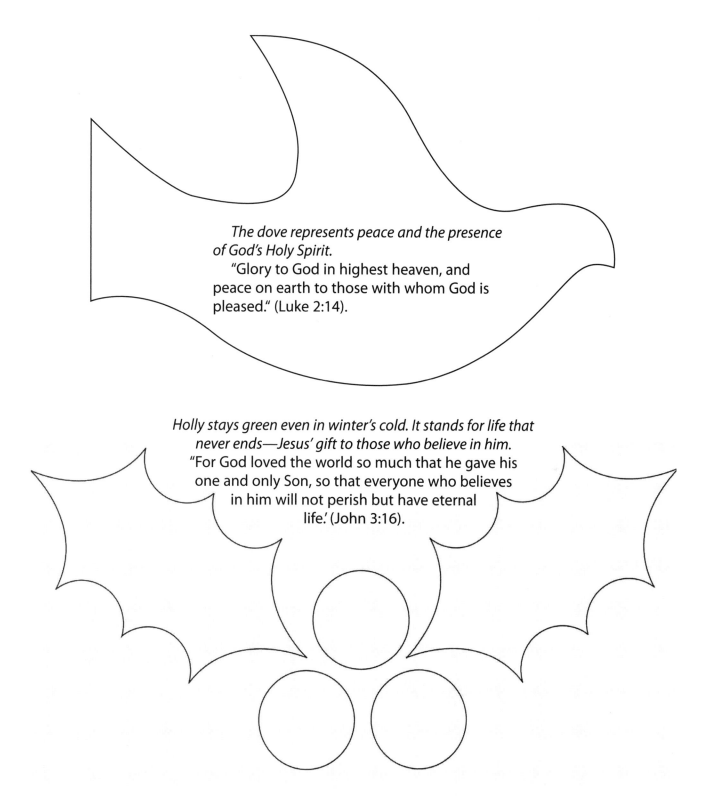

The dove represents peace and the presence of God's Holy Spirit.
"Glory to God in highest heaven, and peace on earth to those with whom God is pleased." (Luke 2:14).

Holly stays green even in winter's cold. It stands for life that never ends—Jesus' gift to those who believe in him.
"For God loved the world so much that he gave his one and only Son, so that everyone who believes in him will not perish but have eternal life." (John 3:16).

Permission to photocopy this handout granted for local church use. Copyright © Lois Keffer.
Published in *All-in-One Sunday School Volume 2* by Group Publishing, Inc., 1515 Cascade Ave., Loveland, CO 80538.

SYMBOLS OF CHRISTMAS

God's Son became a tiny baby who slept in a feeding box, not in a palace.

"The Savior—yes, the Messiah, the Lord—has been born today in Bethlehem, the city of David! And you will recognize him by this sign: You will find a baby wrapped snugly in strips of cloth, lying in a manger." (Luke 2:11-12).

Angels praised God and announced peace on earth.

"Suddenly, the angel was joined by a vast host of others—the armies of heaven—praising God and saying, 'Glory to God in highest heaven, and peace on earth to those with whom God is pleased.'" (Luke 2:13-14).

Permission to photocopy this handout granted for local church use. Copyright © Lois Keffer.
Published in *All-in-One Sunday School Volume 2* by Group Publishing, Inc., 1515 Cascade Ave., Loveland, CO 80538.

SYMBOLS OF CHRISTMAS

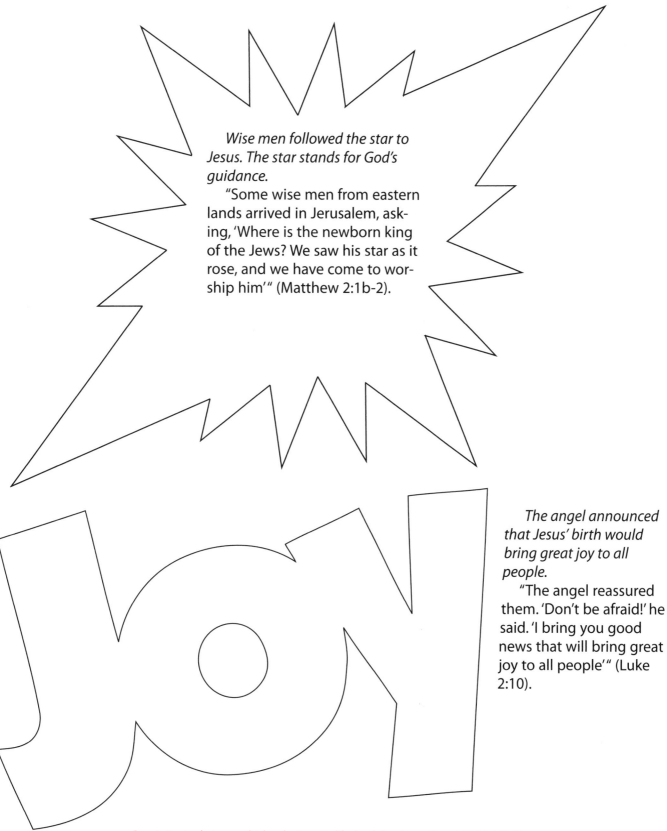

Wise men followed the star to Jesus. The star stands for God's guidance.

"Some wise men from eastern lands arrived in Jerusalem, asking, 'Where is the newborn king of the Jews? We saw his star as it rose, and we have come to worship him'" (Matthew 2:1b-2).

The angel announced that Jesus' birth would bring great joy to all people.

"The angel reassured them. 'Don't be afraid!' he said. 'I bring you good news that will bring great joy to all people'" (Luke 2:10).

Permission to photocopy this handout granted for local church use. Copyright © Lois Keffer.
Published in *All-in-One Sunday School Volume 2* by Group Publishing, Inc., 1515 Cascade Ave., Loveland, CO 80538.

SYMBOLS OF CHRISTMAS

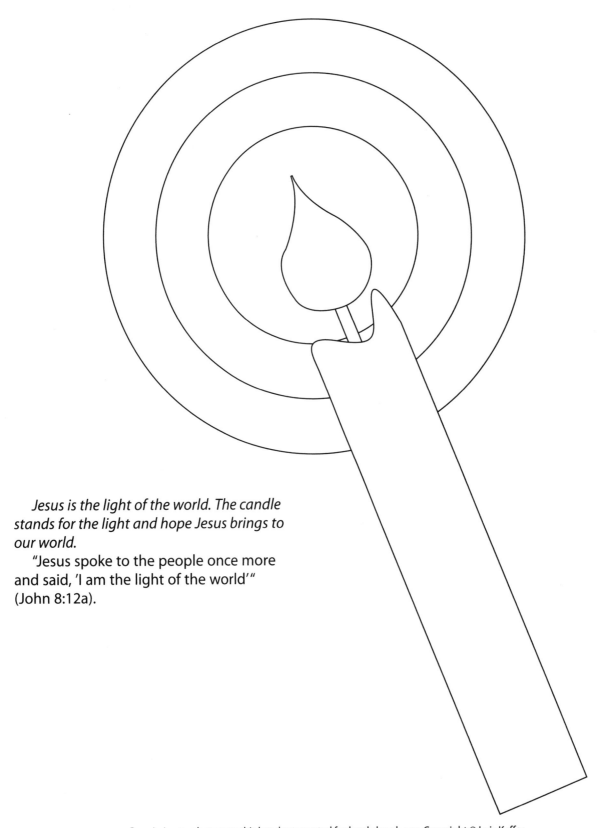

Jesus is the light of the world. The candle stands for the light and hope Jesus brings to our world.

"Jesus spoke to the people once more and said, 'I am the light of the world'" (John 8:12a).

Permission to photocopy this handout granted for local church use. Copyright © Lois Keffer.
Published in *All-in-One Sunday School Volume 2* by Group Publishing, Inc., 1515 Cascade Ave., Loveland, CO 80538.

Jesus, Our Light

LESSON AIM

To help kids understand that ★ Jesus is the light of the world.

OBJECTIVES

Kids or families will
✓ draw self-portraits in the dark,
✓ participate in an active Bible story about how Jesus brought light to a world darkened by sin,
✓ make a craft to remind them that Jesus is the light, and
✓ plan ways to spread Jesus' light.

YOU'LL NEED

❏ paper
❏ pencils or markers
❏ large paper bags
❏ jingle bells
❏ a Bible
❏ tea light candles
❏ matches
❏ scissors
❏ a photocopy of the "Christmas Sing-Along" handout (p. 52)
materials for the learning centers of your choice:
❏ photocopies of the "Candle Paper Sculpture" handouts (pp. 49-50)
 ❏ dark blue, yellow, and white construction paper
 ❏ rulers
 ❏ pencils
❏ photocopies of the "Jesus Is the Light" handout (p. 51)
 ❏ transparent tape
 ❏ pencils
 ❏ votive candles

Teacher Tip

This lesson works well with an intergenerational class. You may wish to invite whole families to join you for this session. Or you might consider using these ideas as the basis for a family Advent night.

all-in-one
SUNDAY
SCHOOL

BIBLE BASIS

John 1:1-9

This beautiful, highly symbolic Scripture details three core beliefs of the Christian faith: that Jesus was with God from the beginning, that Jesus played a key role in Creation, and that Jesus' mission was to bring light and life to those lost in darkness. Christmas is a season of light. Entire cities deck themselves in decorative lighting. Roofs, bushes, and even barren trees boast tiny, sparkling lights of many hues. The warm glow invites us to welcome once again the tiny child who left the pure light of heaven to enter a world made dark by sin. Jesus' advent, though unnoticed by all but a handful of witnesses, cleaves history in two and marks for all people the starting point of God's great plan of redemption.

Isaiah 9:1-2, 6

Don't you love the words of this passage? Imagine the joy Isaiah experienced when God revealed that he would send a great light into the world that would be for all people, not just the Jews. "No more gloom"—hallelujah!

UNDERSTANDING YOUR KIDS

The symbolism of light and darkness is not beyond the grasp of even young children. Kids typically fear dark, shadowy places such as a basement, a closet, or the space under a bed. Kids have also learned to fear the darker side of their own personalities. They know what it's like to throw a tantrum, to get into a fight, and to hurl hurtful words at those they love. With their short span of experience, it's easy for kids to feel that they'll never be any good—that they'll always be the victims of their own sin. Use this lesson to help kids realize that Jesus can replace darkness and fear in their lives with the pure light of his love.

The Lesson

ATTENTION GRABBER

Bag-Heads!

Give each child a sheet of paper, a pencil or marker, and a large paper grocery bag.

Say: **In just a moment, I'm going to give you the opportunity to become something you may never have been before. Congratulations! You're about to become bag-heads!**

Have kids slip the bags over their heads.

Say: **Now that you bag-heads are all in the dark, I'm giving you one minute to draw a self-portrait on the paper in front of you. No peeking! Ready? Go!**

After one minute, call time by shaking the jingle bells. Have kids write their initials in tiny letters on the back of their portraits. Then collect the paper bags, pencils or markers, and portraits.

Say: **I must say, you're a better-looking group now than you were a moment ago! It's nice to see your smiling faces. Now let's see if we can tell whose faces are represented in these portraits I'm holding.**

Hold up the portraits one by one and let kids guess who each portrait represents. Then ask:

♦ **What made it easy or difficult to recognize these portraits?** (We're not good artists; we drew them with bags over our heads.)

♦ **If you'd never met anyone in this class, how could you figure out who's who from these portraits?** (We couldn't, because the portraits aren't that good; we could, because some people drew special things like glasses or braces.)

Say: **These portraits aren't too helpful—they leave us in the dark. After all, you drew them in the dark. There was a time long ago when people felt "in the dark" about God, too. But God didn't keep his people in the dark. Listen to this promise that God spoke through the prophet Isaiah.**

Read Isaiah 9:2, 6. Then ask:

♦ **Who is this light that God sent into the world?** (Jesus; God's Son.)

Teacher Tip

Make absolutely sure you use only roomy paper bags.

DARKNESS TO LIGHT

Long ago, before God created the world, there was nothing but darkness. Then God said, "Let there be light!" *Take off your bags.* And God began creating our beautiful world. God filled the world with wonderful things—beaches and birds, marshes and mountains, whales and snails, dogs and frogs and polliwogs! And last of all, God created people. God made Adam and put him in a beautiful garden. But God saw that Adam needed a friend, so God created Eve. *Go stand next to another student.*

God and Adam and Eve enjoyed being together in the garden. But one day Eve disobeyed God and ate fruit from a special tree. Suddenly Adam and Eve wanted to hide from God. *Put your bags over your heads and sit down.*

Adam and Eve's sin made God sad. God told them to leave the beautiful garden where they lived. Then another terrible thing happened: One of Adam's sons killed the other son. *Press your fists against your partner's fists.*

Soon sin and darkness were all over the world. Most people didn't love God. (Turn off the lights.) *Wrap your arms around your knees.* People became selfish and wicked and mean. *Turn your back on anyone who's close to you and pound your fists on the floor three times.*

Sometimes God sent special people into the world to teach about his love. People would listen. *Raise your head.* And sometimes they would understand and ask God to forgive them for the wrong things they'd done. *Fold your hands as if you're praying.* And, for a little while, God's light would shine. (Flip the lights on.) *Raise your bag halfway off your head.*

But most people kept on sinning. (Turn the lights off again.) *Pull your bag back over your head.* God was sad because he wanted everyone to live in the light of his love.

Then one day God decided to send into the world a light that would never go out. (Light a candle, and then take the bag off one student's head. Give that student a candle and light it.) That light was God's Son, Jesus. (Remove another bag, give that student a candle, and light it. Repeat this process until you've removed all the bags and everyone has a glowing candle.)

Jesus came to earth as a tiny baby. He was born in a stable and was placed in a bed of hay. He grew up and ate and slept and studied and worked. Jesus showed us what God is like.

Jesus taught that God loves us and wants us to love each other. *Form a circle.* Jesus said that our sin separates us from God—*blow out your candles*—but that we can ask God to forgive us. Then God will take the sin from our hearts and put his love there instead. (Light the candles of the students on both sides of you.) Jesus taught us to pass God's love on to others. *Pass the flame around the circle.* And Jesus taught that someday we'll live together in heaven where the light from God's face is the only light we'll need. *Hold your candles up.*

BIBLE STUDY

Darkness to Light (John 1:1-9; Isaiah 9:1-2, 6)

Redistribute the paper grocery bags. Have kids scatter around the room so they're as far from each other as possible. Then tell them to put on the bags.

Say: **Today we're going to learn that ★ Jesus is the light of the world. Listen carefully for instructions as I tell the story. Freeze as you are and don't move or make any sounds until I**

tell you to.

Read the "Darkness to Light" script on the previous page. Read the italicized instructions aloud as part of the story. Follow the directions in parentheses but don't read them aloud.

After you've finished the story, have kids blow out their candles and place their paper bags and candles in a corner of the room. Then ask:

♦ **How was this Christmas story different from other Christmas stories you've heard?** (It started with Creation; it explained why we needed Jesus to come.)

♦ **Why did we need a Savior to come to earth?** (So we could have our sins forgiven; so we could know what God is like.)

♦ **How is not knowing Jesus like being in the dark?** (You feel bad because of your sins; you don't have love and joy in your heart.)

♦ **How does Jesus bring light to our lives?** (He shows us how to live; he takes away our sin; he helps us love each other.)

♦ **What questions do you have about how or why Jesus came to earth?** Discuss as a group any questions that kids raise.

♦ **What customs do we have at Christmastime that remind us that ★ Jesus is the light of the world?** (We put lights on our houses and Christmas trees; we light Advent candles.)

Say: **At Christmastime, we sometimes get so busy that we forget what we're really celebrating. Today we're going to stay focused on the fact that ★ Jesus is the light of the world. And we're going to have fun doing it!**

Teacher Tip

You may want to play soft, instrumental Christmas music as you read the story. As you light the candles, model quiet, calm behavior. Encourage the children to use both hands to carefully hold the lighted candles in front of them.

LIFE APPLICATION

Celebrate-the-Light Learning Centers

Choose one or both of these Advent and Christmas learning-centers. Each is easy to prepare and fun for kids as well as adults. And each center allows participants to actively explore the important truth that ★ Jesus is the light of the world.

Introduce the learning centers. Allow participants to choose where they'd like to begin. Encourage adults and older kids to work together with younger kids to help them complete their projects. If you have time, let participants do both projects; but if you don't have time, offer to send home photocopies of the handouts explaining the project participants didn't have time to complete.

♦ **Candle Paper Sculpture**—Photocopy the "Candle Paper Sculpture" handouts. Photocopy the candle pattern onto white paper. Photocopy the flame pattern onto yellow paper. You'll need one candle pattern and one flame pattern for each participant who chooses this craft. Set out scissors, rulers, pencils, and sheets of dark blue construction paper. Participants will cut and assemble the pieces to make a three-dimensional paper sculpture of a glowing candle.

♦ **Luminarias**—Set out photocopies of the "Jesus Is the Light" handout, scissors, tape, pencils, and votive candles. Participants will make luminarias—small bags that glow with the light of a small candle. Tradition says that several luminarias along a road or sidewalk light the way for the wise men.

Announce when there are five minutes of working time left, then two minutes, then one. When you call time with the jingle bells, have participants gather their projects and sit in a circle.

COMMITMENT

Show and Tell

Say: **Form trios with people who are sitting near you. Show the projects you've made and tell how you'll use them.**

Allow trios to share. Then ring the jingle bells to get everyone's attention.

Say: **Today we've learned that ★ Jesus is the light of the world. Listen to these words from the book of Isaiah: "There will be no more gloom for those who were in distress...The people walking in darkness have seen a great light; on those living in the land of deep darkness a light has dawned...To us a child is born, to us a son is given"** (Isaiah 9:1a, 2, 6a).

Turn to the members of your trio and tell one way Jesus' light has shined on you. Pause for trios to share. Then invite participants to tell the whole group what someone else in their trios shared.

Now tell one way you'll spread Jesus' light this week. Allow volunteers to share their plans to spread Jesus' light.

CLOSING

Christmas Sing-Along

Form three groups. Give each group one of the songs from the "Christmas Sing-Along" handout. Be sure to give the simpler songs to the groups with the most young children. Have groups practice their songs and then take turns teaching them to the whole group.

Close your sing-along with a round of applause for everyone's effort. Then say: **Let's close with a special Christmas greeting. Step up to someone, shake his or her hand, and say, "Jesus is born." The other person will respond, "The light has come." Then say together, "Shine with God's love!"**

Review the greeting once more. Then invite participants to give the greeting to at least five people before they leave.

CANDLE PAPER SCULPTURE

1. Fold the candle pattern in half on the dotted line. Cut out the candle, including the extension.

2. Fold the flame pattern in half on the dotted line. Cut the flame pattern from A to B, then from C to D. Finally cut slit E.

3. Slip the long strip beneath the flame into the slit near the top of the candle and the extension.

4. Fold a sheet of dark blue construction paper in half lengthwise. Cut half-inch slits at the bottom, three inches from the center fold. Open the paper.

5. Tuck the slits in the candle base into the slits in the blue background paper. Bend the center fold of the candle forward. Bend the center fold of the background back.

A

Slit C

B

Slit D

Extension

Permission to photocopy this handout granted for local church use. Copyright © Lois Keffer. Published in *All-in-One Sunday School Volume 2* by Group Publishing, Inc., 1515 Cascade Ave., Loveland, CO 80538.

CANDLE PAPER SCULPTURE

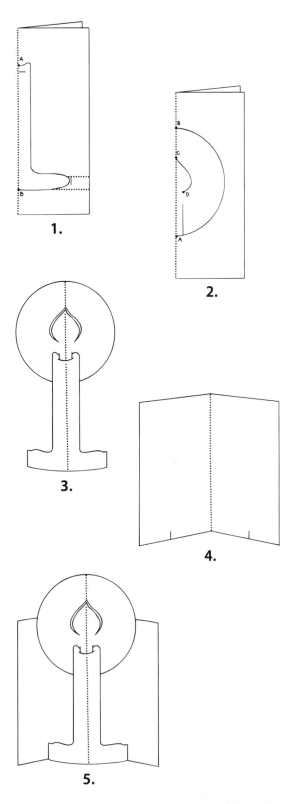

1.

2.

3.

4.

5.

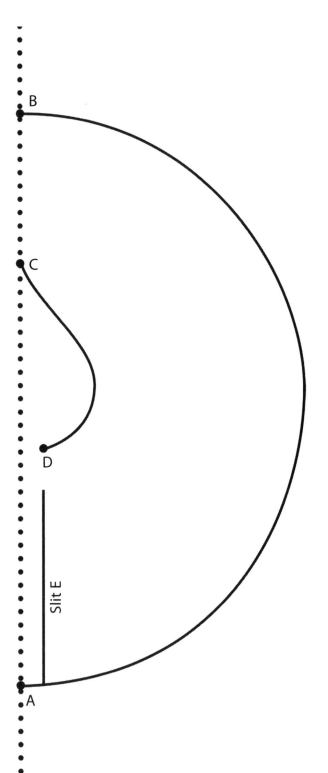

B

C

D

Slit E

A

Permission to photocopy this handout granted for local
church use. Copyright © Lois Keffer. Published in *All-in-One
Sunday School Volume 2* by Group Publishing, Inc.,
1515 Cascade Ave., Loveland, CO 80538.

Tape.

Fold up.

Cut here.

the Light of the world

JESUS

the Light is

Fold up.

Jesus Is
the
LIGHT

A. Use a pencil to poke holes in the star shape.

B. Fold and tape.

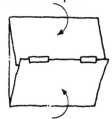

C. Fold up the bottom.

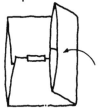

D. Push in the corners.

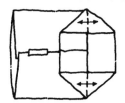

E. Fold the edges over and tape.

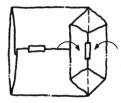

F. Pinch and crease the sides at the bottom.

G. Light a candle inside.

Permission to photocopy this handout granted for local church use. Copyright © Lois Keffer.
Published in *All-in-One Sunday School Volume 2* by Group Publishing, Inc., 1515 Cascade Ave., Loveland, CO 80538.

CHRISTMAS SING-ALONG

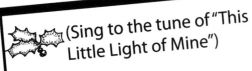 (Sing to the tune of "This Little Light of Mine")

Baby Jesus is mine;
I'm gonna let him shine.
Baby Jesus is mine;
I'm gonna let him shine,
Let him shine, let him shine at
    Christmastime.

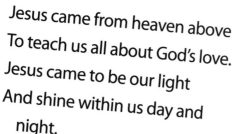 (Sing to the tune of "Jesus Loves Me")

Jesus came from heaven above
To teach us all about God's love.
Jesus came to be our light
And shine within us day and
    night.
Shine, Lord, in me.
Shine, Lord, in me.
Shine, Lord, in me.
Please shine for all to see.

(Sing to the tune of "Jingle Bells")

(verse)
Jesus came to earth
One night long ago;
Way up high in the sky
A big, bright star did glow.
Precious Son of God
Was born on Christmas night.
And now he lives in heaven above
And helps us spread his light.

(chorus)
Shine through me;
Shine through me;
Dear Jesus, shine through me.
Help me spread your light around
For all the world to see.
Shine through me;
Shine through me;
Dear Jesus, shine through me.
Help me spread your light around
For all the world to see.

Permission to photocopy this handout granted for local church use. Copyright © Lois Keffer.
Published in *All-in-One Sunday School Volume 2* by Group Publishing, Inc., 1515 Cascade Ave., Loveland, CO 80538.

LESSON AIM

To help kids understand that ★ God can make us clean inside.

OBJECTIVES

Kids will

✓ tell what they would do if they were kings or queens,
✓ learn how a young king turned his people back to God,
✓ discover how God can make them clean inside, and
✓ discover that God's Word is their greatest treasure.

YOU'LL NEED

❑ foil-covered chocolate coins*
❑ markers
❑ paper
❑ cellophane tape
❑ a hammer
❑ a bowl of charcoal chips
❑ a bowl of marbles or wrapped gum balls*
❑ newsprint
❑ a dishpan of warm, soapy water
❑ a towel
❑ a Bible
❑ photocopies of the "God's Treasure" handout (p. 60)
❑ scissors
Always check for allergies before serving snacks.

BIBLE BASIS

2 Chronicles 33:1–35:19

Josiah was crowned king of Judah when he was 8 years old. Both Josiah's father, Amon, and his grandfather, Manasseh, had led the people of Judah in idol worship. Manasseh's sin resulted

all-in-one
SUNDAY
SCHOOL

in his capture, exile, and imprisonment by the Assyrian army. Manasseh eventually humbled himself before God, received forgiveness, and regained his kingship. On his return to Jerusalem, Manasseh ordered the destruction of idols and led the people in worshipping Jehovah God. After Manasseh's death, Amon took the throne and plunged the nation back into idol worship, sinning even more than his father had done. Amon was killed in his palace by his own officers, and the crown passed to his 8-year-old son.

Despite his tender age and the evil example set by his father, Josiah "did what the Lord said was right." When he was 16 years old, he began worshipping the true God. He rid the whole country of idols and set about rebuilding and restoring the temple. A priest working in the temple found a long-lost scroll containing the law given through Moses. When the young king heard the words of the Law, he tore his clothes in grief for the sins of his nation. The king stood in the temple and read the Law to his people; then he made a covenant to follow God's commands. A short time later, Josiah led his people in the greatest Passover celebration since the time of Samuel.

Josiah was a rare leader among the kings of Israel and Judah. His dedication to God ignited a new faith and a new covenant. God used his servant Josiah to give the people of Judah a new beginning.

Psalm 51:1-2, 10

God loves to hear the repentant cry of his people. He loves us even more than he hates the rotten things we do. God always stands ready to forgive us, make us clean inside, and renew our relationship with him.

UNDERSTANDING YOUR KIDS

An 8-year-old king-boy—will your kids love that! If they were given an opportunity to rule, it wouldn't be long before they'd come up with a great agenda. Rather than "a chicken in every pot," today's kids might legislate a Walt Disney World in every state and a Wii in every home. What a great surprise it will be for your kids to discover that this young ruler had far greater things than amusements on his mind.

There are two positive things for your kids to discover in this lesson. The first is that kids are never too young to make a difference. The second is that when they realize they've offended God, they need to make things right immediately. God is willing to forgive their sins, both purposeful and inadvertent, and make them clean inside.

 # The Lesson

ATTENTION GRABBER

If I Were King

Before class, hide foil-covered chocolate coins around the room. Be sure you hide at least one for each child. To one of the coins tape a slip of paper on which you've written, "Congratulations, Your Majesty!"

Gather kids in a group and say: **I've hidden treasure all around this room. In just a moment I'll let you look for it. Don't pick up more than one piece of treasure. When you've found your piece, bring it back here and sit down. One of the treasures has a special message on it. If you find the treasure with a message, don't tell anyone what it says. Just bring it to me. Are you ready to be treasure hunters? Go!**

When everyone has found a coin, call the group together. Have the child whose coin has the special message come and stand by you. Hold up the coin and read the message to the class.

Then say: **I guess this makes you our ruler. What's your first command?**

If the child is shy or gives a command that seems inappropriate, whisper that he or she might order everyone to eat their treasure. Then ask:

♦ **Suppose you were suddenly to become the ruler of this country; what would you do?** (Make everyone give me chocolate; get homes for all the homeless people.)

♦ **How about the rest of you? What would you do if you suddenly became king or queen?** (Take a world tour; move to a palace; help poor people.)

♦ **What would make you a good king or queen?** (I would be fair and kind; I would tell people about God.)

♦ **What would make you a bad king or queen?** (If I took everyone's money; if I treated my friends and family better than everyone else.)

Say: **Believe it or not, today's Bible story is about a boy who became a king when he was 8 years old. And he turned out to be not just a good king, but a great one! This young king found a treasure, just as we found treasure here today. Let's find out about the treasure he found and what a difference it made in his life and his kingdom.**

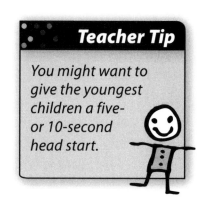

Teacher Tip

You might want to give the youngest children a five- or 10-second head start.

The Little King Who Made a Big Difference
(2 Chronicles 33:23–34:33)

Before class, write "The Little King Who Made a Big Difference" on a sheet of paper.

Help kids form pairs. For this activity it's not necessary to pair younger kids with older ones. Have the pairs sit in a large circle. Set out markers, sheets of paper, and cellophane tape.

Say: **We're going to illustrate this story with the quick-draw method. I'll stand in front of a pair and read a part of the story. One partner will quickly draw a picture describing what I read. Then the other partner will run to this wall** (indicate a blank wall) **and tape the picture to the wall. If I come to your pair more than once, the drawer and the taper may change roles. Don't worry about making fancy pictures; stick figures are fine. Just draw something that will help everyone remember what happens in the story.**

I'll put up the first paper with the title of our story. Who can read it?

Tape the title paper to the wall. Then read "The Little King Who Made a Big Difference" from the next page as you walk around the circle, pausing in front of each pair. Pace the story carefully, waiting just a few seconds between each segment. It's fine to go to the next pair as the previous pair finishes its picture and attaches it to the wall.

After the last picture is in place on the wall, invite kids to join you in front of the pictures. Have kids retell the story by explaining their pictures. Then ask:

♦ **What made Josiah a good king?** (He followed God; he made the people stop worshipping idols.)

♦ **What was the great treasure in this story?** (The book of God's law.)

♦ **What happened when the people of Judah heard what was written in the scroll?** (It made them realize what they'd done wrong; it made them stop sinning and begin to worship God.)

Say: ★ **God can make us clean inside. And that's just what he did for King Josiah and the people of Judah. They had gotten off to a bad start by worshipping idols. But when they found out what was right, they asked God's forgiveness and promised to obey God from then on. So the people got a fresh start.**

A new year is a fresh start for us. But God can give us a fresh start any time. Let's see what we can do to make a fresh start like Josiah did.

THE LITTLE KING WHO MADE A BIG DIFFERENCE

1. King Amon was a wicked man who taught the people of Judah to worship idols. One day he was killed by his own soldiers.

2. Then his young son, Josiah, became king. Josiah was only 8 years old.

3. Josiah worked and studied hard. He wanted to be a good king. When Josiah was 16, he began to worship the true God.

4. Josiah told the people to destroy all the idols in the land. The people obeyed their young king.

5. Josiah ordered the priests to rebuild and repair the temple. Everyone worked hard to make God's house a beautiful place again.

6. One day a priest who was working in the temple found a scroll that had been lost for many, many years. God's laws were written in the scroll.

7. The priest took the scroll to young King Josiah. When Josiah heard God's laws, he knew that his people had broken every law. He felt sad.

8. Josiah called the people to the temple and read God's laws so everyone could hear. The king promised to obey the Law. The people promised to obey, too.

9. Josiah and the people felt sad that they had disobeyed God. When God saw that they were sad and heard their promises to obey, he forgave their sins and made them clean inside.

10. Josiah was one of the greatest kings of Judah. He treasured God's Word and loved God with all his heart and soul and strength.

LIFE APPLICATION

Sad for This, Glad for That

Before class, hit a few charcoal briquettes with a hammer so they shatter into small pieces. Place the pieces in a bowl. Put glass marbles or wrapped gum balls in a second bowl. You'll need enough charcoal chips and marbles or gum balls for each child to have two of each.

Set the bowls together in the center of a table. Place a sheet of newsprint in front of each bowl. Have a dishpan of warm, soapy water and a towel nearby, out of sight.

Say: **When we want to make a fresh start, it's good to stop and think about the good things we've done, as well as the bad things.**

Stand in front of the table and have kids form a line behind you. Pick up a marble or gum ball and say: **I'm glad that I** (name one good thing you did this year). Drop the marble or gum ball on the sheet of newsprint.

Then pick up a charcoal chip and say: **I'm sad that I** (name one thing you did that you felt sorry about). Drop the charcoal chip on the other sheet of newsprint.

Turn and face the kids. Say: **I'd like you to do just what I did. If you want to, you can just say, "I'm glad that…" and "I'm sad that…" and then finish the sentences in your head. Or, you can say what you did out loud. It's up to you. Either way is okay.**

After everyone has been through the line once, invite kids to go through the line again if they wish. It's fine if some kids choose to go a second time and others choose not to. You may want to lead the second round as you did the first.

Then gather everyone around the table and ask:

♦ **What happened to your hands when you named the things you were sad about?** (The charcoal turned them black; they got dirty.)

♦ **How does the charcoal feel on your hands?** (Icky; I want to get them clean.)

♦ **How is that like how it feels to have sin in your life?** (You feel bad about it.)

Say: **Listen to these verses from the Bible.** Read aloud Psalm 51:1-2, 10.

Set out the dishpan of warm, soapy water and the towel. Have kids take turns washing and drying their hands. As children put their hands in the water, have them repeat Psalm 51:2 after you: "Wash me clean from my guilt. Purify me from my sin."

When everyone has washed and dried their hands, say: **Doesn't that feel better? Just as the soapy water cleaned our hands, ★ God can make us clean inside. Then we're ready for a fresh start, just like King Josiah and the people of Judah.**

Promise kids that they can take their gum balls or marbles home after class.

COMMITMENT

God's Treasure

Ask:

♦ **What treasure helped Josiah and his people make a new start?** (The book of God's law.)

♦ **Why is God's Word a great treasure?** (Because it teaches us about God; because it tells us what God wants us to do.)

Say: **We're going to make treasure boxes to remind us of the new beginning God gave the people of Judah and the new beginning God is willing to give us when we ask him to forgive our sins.**

Distribute photocopies of the "God's Treasure" handout and scissors. Have kids cut out and roll the scroll containing Psalm 51:1-2, 10. Then demonstrate how to cut and fold the treasure box. The box can be made from the square pattern on the handout or from a 6-inch square of wrapping paper.

Have kids write their initials on the bottom of the finished treasure boxes and then tuck the scrolls inside.

CLOSING

Treasures to Keep

Have kids stand in a circle holding their treasure boxes. Ask:

♦ **What will these treasure boxes remind you of?** (That God can make us clean inside; that God can give us a fresh start; that God can take away our sins.)

Say: **Let's bow our heads and pray a prayer of thanks because ★ God can make us clean inside.**

Pray: **Dear Lord, thank you for the treasure of your Word. Thank you for taking away our sins and making us clean inside. And thank you for giving us a fresh start. In Jesus' name, amen.**

Encourage kids to tell their families about their treasure boxes and to keep the treasure boxes as reminders that God can make them clean inside.

Teacher Tip

Practice folding the treasure box two or three times before class. You may want to train two or three kids to be helpers. Take heart—making the box is much simpler than it looks! It's based on the familiar "salt cellar" or "May basket" pattern many kids are familiar with.

1.

2.

3.

4.

5.

5.

GOD'S TREASURE

1. Fold the square diagonally both ways; then open it flat with the plain side up.

2. Fold all four corners to the center.

3. Turn the square over and fold all four corners to the center again.

4. Fold all the points outward so they extend beyond the square.

5. Turn the square over. Fold the center points back to the outside points.

6. Pinch each top point from the outside, causing the points to stand up and fold at the top.

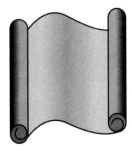

"Have mercy on me, O God, because of your unfailing love. Because of your great compassion, blot out the stain of my sins. Wash me clean from my guilt. Purify me from my sin. Create in me a clean heart, O God. Renew a loyal spirit within me." (Psalm 51:1-2, 10).

Permission to photocopy this handout granted for local church use. Copyright © Lois Keffer.
Published in *All-in-One Sunday School Volume 2* by Group Publishing, Inc., 1515 Cascade Ave., Loveland, CO 80538.

LESSON AIM

To help kids understand that ★ Jesus is our good shepherd.

OBJECTIVES

Kids will

✓ realize Jesus is kind, loving, and wants the best for them,
✓ understand Jesus can be close to them when they feel separated and lost,
✓ trust Jesus to guide them, and
✓ make a commitment to follow Jesus.

YOU'LL NEED

❑ blindfolds
❑ an older girl to play Woolina
❑ a photocopy of "Woolina's Mask" (p. 68)
❑ a dowel
❑ scissors
❑ newsprint
❑ markers
❑ tape
❑ Bibles
❑ photocopies of the "Psalm Pstarter" handout (p. 69)
❑ pencils

BIBLE BASIS

Psalm 23

This psalm needs to be read from a sheep's point of view. Notice the sheep's delight in its wonderful shepherd. With the shepherd close by, the sheep had no fear—even though the canyons leading to the high grassy meadows were difficult to climb and full of predators.

Jesus welcomes this kind of total dependence and trust

61

from us. Society teaches us to be strong and self-reliant, but Scripture shows us we're truly strong and safe only when we're close to our Good Shepherd.

John 10:1-15

The sheep know the shepherd's voice, and he knows their names. What a wonderful assurance for kids to realize Jesus knows them each by name. The challenge is to learn to listen for his voice.

UNDERSTANDING YOUR KIDS

Who doesn't remember at least one terrifying childhood experience that had to do with getting lost? First there's panic, then loneliness, then a sinking realization that there's probably little we can do to "get found." One lost-in-the-mall experience teaches kids the importance of sticking close to the person in charge.

Younger kids' biggest worry is they'll somehow be separated from their parents. They'll find comfort in knowing they have a Good Shepherd who cares for them and will always be with them, even when mom and dad are far away.

Older kids are anxious to grow up and assert their independence—that's natural and healthy. But they need to see true maturity means recognizing how much we need to rely on God. And it means following in the footsteps of our infinitely wise and loving Good Shepherd.

☻ The Lesson

ATTENTION GRABBER

Lost Sheep

Before class, create one mask using a photocopy of "Woolina's Mask" from page 68 and tape it to a dowel. Ask an older girl to volunteer to play the role of Woolina.

Use chairs to fence off one corner of the classroom as a "sheepfold." Make sure the fold has an entrance no bigger than the width of one chair. Explain that at night, sheep always come into the fold where they are protected from wolves, mountain lions, and robbers.

Blindfold all of the children. One by one, take the blindfolded "sheep" to the "wilderness"—places far away from the fold. Take older kids farther into the wilderness than younger kids—outside the class area. Make things more confusing by inventing twists and turns in your path as you lead them away. Have kids spin around three times and then try to find their way back to the fold.

If kids seem totally confused about how to get back to the fold, take them by the shoulders and gently turn them in the right direction. As you guide them, say: **This way, [name]. This is the way to the fold.**

When everyone is gathered in the fold, have kids remove their blindfolds. Ask:

♦ **How did it feel trying to find your way back here?** (Scary; confusing; it was fun.)

♦ **How is this like what happens to you in real life when you get lost?** (I feel scared and don't know which way to go; somebody usually comes along to help.)

♦ **How is this different from really being lost?** (I knew I was really in Sunday school; all I had to do was pull off my blindfold.)

♦ **How did you feel when the shepherd came along to help you?** (I felt comforted; I liked hearing my name and knowing you were there to guide me.)

♦ **How is Jesus like a shepherd to us?** (He knows us by name; he knows what's best for us and wants to help us and keep us safe.)

Say: **Today we're going to learn more about our Good Shepherd and about sheep. Tell me what you know about sheep.** Allow kids to respond. **You really know a lot! I'm going to introduce you to someone who will tell you more about sheep, and she ought to know because she is one! Please welcome my friend Woolina.**

Have the child who volunteered to play Woolina hold the up the mask and read the "Meet Woolina!" story on the next page.

> **Teacher Tip**
>
> *If your class is mostly older kids, make the Lost Sheep activity more lively by adding a wolf. Blindfold the wolf and lead him or her farther from the fold than any of the sheep. The wolf howls when it tags a sheep, and then the sheep must play dead.*

63

MEET WOOLINA!

Baa!

My name is Woolina. I'm a sheep. A lot of people think sheep are really dumb. They're right! Turkeys may be a little dumber, but sheep are pretty dumb.

Do you know I could die of thirst with a pool of water just over the next hill? Sheep can't smell water like other animals can. I have no sense of direction. I couldn't find my way home if I had to. I don't even have enough sense to come in out of a storm!

I have no defenses at all. If a wolf or a mountain lion comes at me, I just stand there and wait to be eaten.

I'm not too smart about the way I eat, either. I've got really great teeth (show your teeth), and I can pull grass right up by the roots. My flock will often strip a field bare in just a few days and ruin the grazing there for years to come.

The most embarrassing thing about being a sheep is falling down and not being able to get up. If I roll over on my back too far I get stuck, and I just have to stay that way until help comes along.

You probably wonder how a dumb animal like me ever survives. Good question! The truth is, I depend on my shepherd for everything—food, water, shelter, and protection. I wouldn't make it through a week without my shepherd.

I know you humans think you're a lot smarter than I am. But I've seen that humans need a lot of help, too. I think you're just pulling the wool over your own eyes. I don't want to be "baad," but it seems to me that you need a shepherd just as much as I do!

Have kids give Woolina a round of applause. Then ask:

♦ **What did Woolina say that surprised you?** (Sheep could fall over and not be able to get up; they can't smell water like other animals.)

♦ **Woolina thinks people need shepherds, too; why would people need a shepherd?** (People sometimes get sick and need help; people face big problems in life and need the help of someone wise and strong.)

♦ **What kind of shepherd do you think Woolina would like to have?** (Someone who is patient; strong; brave; knows where good food is.)

As kids give their answers to the last question, list them on a sheet of newsprint taped to the wall. Then ask:

♦ **What kind of shepherd would you like to have?** (Someone who understands me and cares about me; someone I can turn to when I'm scared.)

List these answers on the newsprint, as well.

Ask:

♦ **The Bible tells us about someone who wants to be our good shepherd; can anyone who is younger than 6 years old tell me who that is?** (Jesus.)

Say: ★ **Jesus is our good shepherd. Let's see how this good shepherd compares to the list we've made here.**

BIBLE STUDY

The Good Shepherd (Psalm 23; John 10:1-15)

Gather all the kids into the fold. Ask for one volunteer to be a robber and one to be a wolf. The rest of the kids will be sheep. Whenever you mention the word *shepherd*, all the sheep are to smile and say "baa!" But the robber and wolf are to turn around and hide their faces. Tell kids to listen carefully for their parts in the Bible story and to do exactly what it says.

Read John 10:1-15 in your best storytelling manner. Be sure to use a version of the Bible kids will easily understand. Emphasize "shepherd" so kids can catch their cues.

After the story, have kids sit in a circle.

Ask:

♦ **What did you like best about the good shepherd?** (I like it that he knows all the sheep by name; I like him for protecting the sheep from wolves and robbers.)

♦ **How would you feel if you had a shepherd like that?** (Safe; happy.)

♦ **How is Jesus like the good shepherd in this story?** (He cares for us and gives us the things we need; he gave his life for us.)

♦ **In the story, the good shepherd protected the sheep from wolves and robbers. What kinds of scary things can Jesus help us face today?** (Getting separated from mom or dad; facing mean kids at school; getting sick.)

♦ **How is having Jesus in your life like having a good shepherd?** (I can turn to him in prayer when I feel scared or kids are bugging me.)

Now have kids turn to Psalm 23. Little ones who can't read yet will enjoy looking on with older readers.

Say: **Today we're going to do something fun and different with this psalm.**

> **Teacher Tip**
>
> *If you have plenty of time and your kids are enjoying this activity, let groups teach their motions to each other. Then have kids practice performing the whole psalm. Encourage kids to perform the psalm for their parents later in the day.*

Have kids form six groups. A group can be as few as one or two kids. Include older and younger kids in each group.

Assign each of the six groups one verse of Psalm 23, and have them make up their own sign language to tell what the verse says. Encourage kids to use their whole bodies to express the meanings of their verses.

Allow a couple of minutes for kids to plan. Then bring everyone together, and line up the groups in verse order. Read the psalm aloud and have kids perform their verses.

Ask:

♦ **How did you feel as you were making up the motions?** (Happy; excited.)

♦ **How does performing this psalm make you think about Jesus?** (It makes me love him; I want to stay close to him; it makes me glad there's someone strong who will always be there for me.)

Say: **I hope you'll remember the good feelings you get from this psalm. Also remember the psalm doesn't promise that nothing scary will ever happen to us. But it does promise our Good Shepherd will be with us through good times and bad times. ★ Jesus is our good shepherd.**

LIFE APPLICATION

Psalms for the Shepherd

Give kids each a photocopy of the "Psalm Pstarter" handout and a pencil.

Say: **You can write a psalm of your own and tell Jesus how you feel about him. We'll be using the sheep pictures later.**

Circulate among kids as they're working, giving them ideas and encouragement, and helping those who are having trouble. Have kids share their finished psalms. Praise them for the love they expressed and for their creativity.

COMMITMENT

Jesus' Flock

Draw kids' attention to the characteristics of a good shepherd that they listed on the newsprint earlier. Let young readers raise their hands if they can read a word on the list. Have them come up individually, point to a word, and read it.

For each characteristic ask:

♦ **In what way is Jesus like this?**

When you've been through the whole list, ask the class:

♦ **How do you feel knowing ★ Jesus is your good shepherd?**

Ask a 7- or 8-year-old to come up and draw a picture of

Teacher Tip

You may choose to do this activity in pairs, having older kids work with younger ones. If you have a very young class, you may wish to write the psalm as a whole class on a sheet of newsprint.

Jesus on a sheet of newsprint. Have an older child title the picture "Our Good Shepherd." Give kids each a pair of scissors and a pencil. Then have kids cut out one of the sheep from their "Psalm Pstarter" handouts.

Say: **Write your name on your sheep. Then bring it up here and tape it on the picture close to Jesus.**

Pass out strips of tape as kids bring up their sheep. When the "flock" has been assembled on the newsprint, ask:

♦ **What can you do to stay close to the Good Shepherd this week?** (Sing songs that remind me of Jesus; pray; read the Bible or listen to Bible stories; ask Jesus to be with me in scary times.)

Have kids each cut out the other sheep from the "Psalm Pstarter" handout and write on it one thing they'll do to stay close to Jesus this week. Younger kids can draw instead of write. Encourage kids to show their sheep to their parents and discuss their plans for staying close to the Good Shepherd.

CLOSING

Thanks to the Shepherd

Have kids sing the simple round "The Lord Is My Shepherd" or another simple song about Jesus. Then have them huddle for a closing prayer, thanking Jesus for caring for them and being their good shepherd.

WOOLINA'S MASK

Cut out this mask and the holes for the eyes. You may want to glue the mask to cardboard and tape a ruler or dowel on the back for a handle.

Permission to photocopy this handout granted for local church use. Copyright © Lois Keffer.
Published in *All-in-One Sunday School Volume 2* by Group Publishing, Inc., 1515 Cascade Ave., Loveland, CO 80538.

PSALM PSTARTER

Write your own psalm by completing these sentences.

Because the Lord is …

I will never …

Lord, you are …

Thank you, for I will always …

Permission to photocopy this handout granted for local church use. Copyright © Lois Keffer.
Published in *All-in-One Sunday School Volume 2* by Group Publishing, Inc., 1515 Cascade Ave., Loveland, CO 80538.

LESSON AIM

To help kids understand that ★ God is always ready to forgive us.

OBJECTIVES

Kids will

✓ experience unfairness in a game,
✓ discover why the people of Jericho disliked Zacchaeus,
✓ learn that love and forgiveness can melt bad feelings, and
✓ understand why it's important to forgive.

YOU'LL NEED

❏ a plastic tablecloth
❏ 5 containers of progressively larger sizes
❏ masking tape
❏ bags of jelly beans*
❏ a ¼-cup measuring cup or scoop
❏ a roll of bathroom tissue or adding machine tape
❏ Bibles
❏ ice cubes
❏ photocopies of the "Heart of Forgiveness" handout (p. 78)
❏ scissors
❏ red and white construction paper
Always check for allergies before serving snacks.

BIBLE BASIS

Luke 19:1-10

Zacchaeus was a guy everyone loved to hate. Not only did he collaborate with the hated Roman government as a tax collector, he was crooked to boot! Zacchaeus was the lowest of the low—a greedy villain who didn't care who suffered from his misdeeds. No wonder the crowd expressed shock and

dismay when Jesus said, "Zacchaeus, hurry and come down! I must stay at your house today." Unthinkable! Outrageous! Jesus had really gone too far.

Or had he? Jesus always welcomed sinners who were somehow humbled and broken when confronted by his love. Jesus must've seen something the rest of us miss—the misery and despair of a life out of control, the potential for good, the desperate desire to change. Zacchaeus' change was both immediate and profound. He gave half his wealth to the poor and repaid his victims four times the amount he'd stolen from them.

There's an important lesson here for all Christians: God extends his grace and forgiveness to every man, woman, and child on this earth who approaches in humble repentance. Football has ineligible receivers. God doesn't.

Luke 6:37

In this passage, Jesus makes it clear that for Christians, a willingness to forgive is a requirement, not an option. And that's a tough assignment. If we set high standards of behavior for ourselves, it seems natural to have the same expectations of others. It's important to remember that our self-righteousness is "as filthy rags." God has forgiven our imperfections and we, in turn, must forgive others'.

UNDERSTANDING YOUR KIDS

Most kids—even many Christian kids—think it's okay to nurse a grudge. It seems to kids that friends and enemies just happen. If Katrina was rude to me today, I'll just be rude to her the rest of the week or the rest of the school year or the rest of my life. That's just the way things work out, right? Not!

Children often fail to realize that there's another side to every story. Maybe Katrina is feeling a lot of pressure from her parents to get good grades. Maybe her older sister bit her head off just before they left for school. Maybe Katrina's world is a dark, awful place right now, and the child in your class just happened to be the next person she bumped into.

Kids need to see that sometimes their perceptions about people can be off the mark. To the people of Jericho, Zacchaeus was a dastardly villain. To Jesus he was a miserable creature, desperately in need of compassion and forgiveness. This lesson will help your kids respond with compassion to those who need their forgiveness and love.

The Lesson 😃

ATTENTION GRABBER

Jelly Bean Scene

Spread a clean plastic tablecloth on the floor and set five clean containers of progressively larger sizes on it. Set the smallest container in the front and the largest in the back. For example, the smallest container might be a rinsed tin can, and the largest might be a clean bucket. Mark a starting line with masking tape about two feet from the first container. Leave several inches between containers so that the last container is about four feet behind the first.

As kids arrive, give them each a bag containing 15 jelly beans. Choose a confident child to be the "tax collector." Take the tax collector aside, give him or her a large bag of jelly beans, and explain that he or she is to move the starting line back about a foot after the first round, then about a yard after the second round. Explain that during the discussion time at the end of the game, you'll prompt him or her to take everyone's red jelly beans.

Say: **You'll take turns standing behind the starting line and tossing your jelly beans into the containers. The goal is to drop your first jelly bean into the first container, the second jelly bean into the second container, and so on. We'll play three rounds. You can collect all the jelly beans that go into the right containers. But the tax collector gets to keep all the jelly beans that miss. Ready? Let's play!**

Have kids take turns tossing five beans. Let each player collect the beans that land in the containers. Have the tax collector snatch away the beans that miss. After everyone's had a turn, prompt the tax collector to say, "This game is too easy! I'm gonna fix it," and move the starting line back a foot. After the second round, have the tax collector move the starting line back a yard. If the kids complain, simply play along and say: **I guess we'd better do what the tax collector says—he's [she's] in charge!**

After the third round, call everyone together and have kids show how many jelly beans they've collected. Have the tax collector show how many he or she has collected. Then ask:

♦ **What do you think about this game?** (It was fun; it wasn't fair; it was too hard.)

♦ **Was it fair when the tax collector moved the line? Why or why not?** (No, because it got harder and the tax collector got to keep more beans; no, it gave the tax collector an unfair advantage.)

Say: **Well, I'm sorry to say this, but I think our tax collector has even more bad news.** Prompt the tax collector to demand

and collect everyone's red jelly beans. Then call the tax collector over to you. Say: **These kids seem pretty upset with the way this game turned out. You've got a lot more jelly beans than anyone else.** Hand the tax collector a ¼-cup measuring cup or scoop and say: **We don't want to make any enemies, so I'll help you give everyone a nice big scoop of jelly beans.**

After you've added jelly beans to each child's bag, say: **Today we're going to discover that ★ God is always ready to forgive us—even when we take other people's jelly beans! What happened in our game is a lot like what happens in our Bible story today. Let's set our jelly bean bags over by the wall and see what happens to the nasty, cheating, mean, greedy tax collector in our story.**

Be sure to reserve some jelly beans for the "Hearts of Forgiveness" activity.

BIBLE STUDY

Tax-to-the-Max Zack (Luke 19:1-10)

Say: **First, let's set the stage for our story. At the far end of the room we need to make a tree by having two kids stand on either side of a chair.** Have two volunteers stand on either side of a chair, holding their arms out like branches. Coach them to help "Zacchaeus" (za-KEE-us) climb safely on the chair and back down again during the story. **Now we need someone to play Jesus and stand at the opposite end of the room from the tree. Next we need a person to play Zacchaeus and stand between the tree and Jesus. Zacchaeus was a little guy, so you'll need to get down on your knees.** Position the actors playing Jesus and Zacchaeus. **The rest of you will be the crowd. Stand here near the middle of the road in front of Zacchaeus. Good! You folks in the crowd don't like Zack, so every time I mention his name, you can boo. But you love Jesus, so every time I mention his name, you can clap and cheer. I'll be the narrator. Here we go!**

Read the story "Tax-to-the-Max Zack" on the next page, pausing to coach the actors.

After the story, have kids give themselves a big round of applause. Then gather everyone and ask:

♦ **Why was Zack so unpopular?** (Because he cheated; because he took people's money; because he worked for the Romans.)

♦ **Was it wrong of the people of Jericho to feel the way they did about Zack? Explain.** (No, because he was a rotten guy; no, I probably would have disliked him, too.)

♦ **If you'd been in Jericho that day, how would you have reacted when Jesus announced that he wanted to visit Zack's house?** (I probably would have been surprised; I probably

TAX-TO-THE-MAX ZACK

(based on Luke 19:1-10)

Long ago, in Jesus' time, there lived a man we'll call Tax-to-the-Max Zack. Zack worked for the hated Roman government—that made him a traitor. He was their chief tax collector—that made him really unpopular. And he was as crooked as a cow's hind leg. He always added a little to everyone's tax bill and kept the extra for himself—that made him a cheat. Why, Zack would even cheat a blind widow. This guy was the lowest of the low.

One day the people of Jericho (that's where Zack lived) heard that Jesus was coming to town. The town fairly burst with excitement. Everyone jabbered about Jesus. "I wonder if he'll do a miracle," said some. "I hope he heals my grandmother," said another. "She's been sick for such a long time."

Long before Jesus appeared, a big crowd started to form along the road. Zack was there too, but he got pushed clear to the back. No one was about to make room for Tax-to-the-Max. No sirree. Jesus wouldn't want to get near him anyway—or so everyone thought.

Finally the people could see Jesus walking down the road toward Jericho. Everyone strained to get a look. But Zack was stuck in the back and, being a little guy, couldn't see a thing. Then he noticed a tree just a little way up the road. "I could climb that tree," Zack thought. "Then I could see Jesus, too."

So Zack climbed the tree. "Oh, good!" he thought. "Now I can see Jesus. And he's coming right this way!"

Zack's heart started beating ker-thump, ker-thump, ker-thump! Jesus headed straight for the sycamore tree where Zack was perched. Jesus looked up and said, "Zacchaeus, hurry and come down! I must stay at your house today."

Everyone in the crowd gasped. Even Zack could hardly believe his ears. Jesus wanted to visit him? The crowd began to mumble and complain. "Doesn't Jesus know this man is a sinner? Why would the Lord want to visit Tax-to-the-Max?"

But that's just what Jesus did. And you'd never believe what happened to Zack. He changed—just like that! Jesus' love crept into that mean, nasty heart of his. Jesus must've seen something in Zack that no one else could see. Jesus saw that Zack was sorry for all the wrong things he'd done and all the people he'd hurt. Jesus saw that Zack wanted to be forgiven so he could have a clean heart and new life. Why, Zack stood right up and said to Jesus, "I will give half of my possessions to the poor. And if I have cheated anyone, I will pay back four times more."

A big smile crossed Jesus' face, and he said, "Salvation has come to this house today, because this man also belongs to the family of Abraham. The Son of Man came to find lost people and save them."

Well, if Jesus could save Zack, he could save anyone.

wouldn't have liked it; I might have gotten mad at Jesus.)

♦ **Why do you think Jesus announced in front of the whole crowd that he wanted to go to Zack's house?** (He wanted people to see that he loved everyone; people needed to know that God can forgive everyone.)

♦ **Why do you think visiting with Jesus made such a big change in Zack's life?** (Because he could feel Jesus' love; because he wanted to be like Jesus and be one of Jesus' followers.)

♦ **What can we learn from the story of Zacchaeus?** (That God loves everyone; that God can forgive anybody; that we should realize that bad people sometimes want to change.)

Say: **The people of Jericho probably thought that Zack was rich and happy. But in reality, Zack was rich and miserable. Zack had heard about Jesus' miracles and must have had faith that Jesus could change even his miserable, rotten life. Zack and the people of Jericho learned that ★ God is always ready to forgive us. Let's see what other lessons we can discover from this story.**

LIFE APPLICATION

Wrapped Up and Frozen

Have the child who played Zacchaeus stand in the middle of the class. Have the rest of the kids make a circle around Zacchaeus and begin wrapping him or her with bathroom tissue or adding machine tape.

Say: **We want to wrap Zacchaeus from head to toe to show that Zacchaeus was all wrapped up in sin.** Ask:

♦ **How does sin wrap you up?** (When you do something wrong, you usually have to do something else wrong to cover it up; when you do bad things, people blame you for other things.)

Say: **Pretty soon Zacchaeus was wrapped up by hate, too, because no one liked him. If Zacchaeus had dropped dead, people would probably have cheered. But Jesus was different. Jesus saw how much Zacchaeus was hurting inside. And Jesus wanted to set him free.** Ask:

♦ **How could Zacchaeus be set free from his sin?** (By asking forgiveness; by telling Jesus he was sorry.)

Say: **Listen to what the Bible says about forgiveness.** Have a volunteer read 1 John 1:9 aloud. Then say: **God is the only one who can truly set us free from sin, and ★ God is always ready to forgive us. All we have to do is ask. Zacchaeus, I think it's time for you to break out!** Have everyone help the child playing Zacchaeus burst out of the paper that's holding him or her. Say, "Yes!" and lead the class in a round of applause. Then ask Zacchaeus:

♦ **How did it feel, being all wrapped up?** (Tight; bad.)

♦ **What was it like to break out?** (Cool; it felt good.)

♦ **How do you think the real Zacchaeus felt when his sins were forgiven?** (Free; like a new person; clean.)

♦ **How do you think the people in Jericho felt when they saw what had happened to Zacchaeus?** (Some were probably happy; others might have doubted that it was for real.)

Say: **It isn't always easy to forgive, especially if a person has hurt us in some way.** Have kids form pairs. Give each pair a small ice cube. **Unforgiveness freezes the flow of God's love. Jesus warned us about that. As I read Jesus' words, see how quickly you and your partner can melt your ice cube. You can take turns holding it so no one's hands get too cold.**

As pairs work on melting their ice cubes, read the following passages from an easy-to-understand version of the Bible: Matthew 6:13-15; Luke 6:37; and Colossians 3:13.

As the ice cubes continue to melt, ask:

♦ **What did you learn from these Scriptures?** (That we need to forgive others if we want God to forgive us; that if we don't forgive other people, God won't forgive us.)

♦ **How is melting an ice cube like forgiving someone?** (It melts away bad feelings; it helps people feel warm toward each other.)

♦ **Why should we forgive people who've done bad things?** (Because God is willing to forgive them; because God still loves them, and we should, too.)

Say: **Sometimes we need to ask God to help us see people through Jesus' eyes—through eyes of love. Jesus helped the people of Jericho see the change in Zacchaeus, and he can do the same for us today.**

COMMITMENT

Hearts of Forgiveness

Say: **Let's make something to remind us that forgiveness is a gift from God, a gift that God wants us to pass on to others.**

Distribute photocopies of the "Heart of Forgiveness" handout, scissors, and red and white construction paper. Demonstrate how to use the pattern to cut the red and white paper and how to weave the basket.

As kids work, discuss the topic of forgiveness. Ask questions such as "When is it really hard to forgive someone?" and "How do you feel after you've asked God for forgiveness?"

Have kids sit in a circle with their completed heart baskets in hand. Bring the remaining jelly beans and join kids in the circle. Say: ★ **God is always ready to forgive us, and God expects us to pass his forgiveness along to others.**

Turn to the child on your right, pour a few jelly beans in his or her heart basket, and say: [Name], **God is always ready to forgive you.** Pass the bag of jelly beans to that child and have him or her repeat the process with the next child. Continue until each person has been affirmed.

Say: **Forgiving people who have hurt us is one of the hardest things God asks us to do. I'd like you to close your eyes and take a few quiet moments to think about someone you've had difficulty forgiving. You may want to ask God to help you see that person through Jesus' eyes.** Pause for a few moments. **Keeping your eyes closed, eat one of the jelly beans from your basket. Let that jelly bean represent how God has forgiven you. Now eat another jelly bean to represent the forgiveness that you can pass on to others.**

CLOSING

Full Hearts

Say: **Now you may open your eyes. You'll notice that we started this activity by filling each other's baskets. That's important because God doesn't expect us to forgive from an empty heart. First God fills our hearts with his love and forgiveness; then he asks us to pass that love and forgiveness on to others.**

Have kids stand for prayer. Close with a prayer similar to this one: **Lord, thank you that ★ you're always ready to forgive us. Help us learn to see people through your eyes and to pass your love and forgiveness on to others. In Jesus' name, amen.**

Teacher Tip

Kids love these heart-shaped baskets, but you'll find them a bit more challenging than some other crafts in this book. Practice making the basket before class and have an assistant practice with you. A simpler alternative is to have kids cut hearts from the two bottom corners of an envelope as shown below.

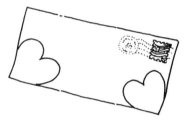

1. Cut the pattern from folded red construction paper and white construction paper.

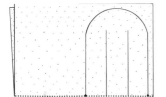 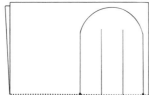

2. Lay the red and white patterns side by side, curved ends up.

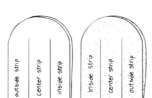

3. Weave the inside red strip through the inside white strip, around the center white strip, and through the outside white strip. Push the red strip up.

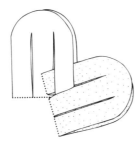

4. Weave the center red strip around the inside white strip, through the center white strip, and around the outside white strip.

5. Weave the outside red strip through the inside white strip, around the center white strip, and through the outside white strip. When the basket is finished, it will resemble a woven, heart-shaped pocket.

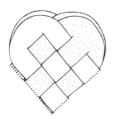

Heart of Forgiveness

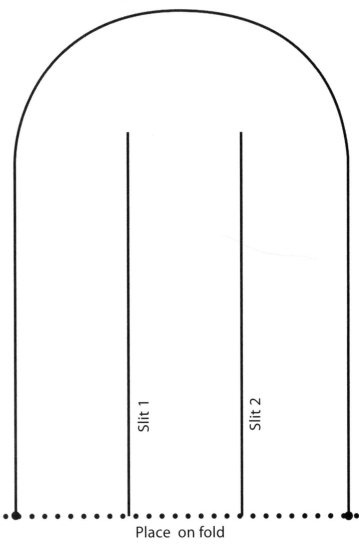

Slit 1

Slit 2

Place on fold

Permission to photocopy this handout granted for local church use. Copyright © Lois Keffer.
Published in *All-in-One Sunday School Volume 2* by Group Publishing, Inc., 1515 Cascade Ave., Loveland, CO 80538.

A Father's Faith

LESSON AIM

To help kids understand that ★ Jesus cares about our families.

OBJECTIVES

Kids or families will

✓ hear how Jesus helped Jairus and his little girl,
✓ discover how family members depend on each other,
✓ make affirmation cards for members of their families, and
✓ reflect upon the need to show love and appreciation to each member of their families.

YOU'LL NEED

❑ balloons
❑ masking tape
❑ large potatoes
❑ bowls of water
❑ bars of soap
❑ paper towels
❑ safety pins
❑ Bible-times costume (optional)
❑ sandwich bags
❑ tablespoons
❑ a bowl of dried cereal*
❑ a bowl of M&M's*
❑ a bowl of raisins*
❑ Bibles
❑ scissors
❑ markers or colored pencils
❑ photocopies of the "From the Bottom of My Heart" handout (p. 88)
❑ photocopies of the "Thanks a Bunch" handout (p. 89)
*Always check for allergies before serving snacks.

> **Teacher Tip**
>
> This lesson works well with an intergenerational class. You may wish to invite whole families to join you for this session.

all-in-one
SUNDAY
SCHOOL

BIBLE BASIS

Mark 5:21-24, 35-43

Desperation drove Jairus to Jesus. Jairus' daughter lay dying and his only hope was in the healing hands of the controversial teacher from Nazareth. What a juicy tidbit of gossip Jairus must have generated when he pushed his way through a crowd and fell at Jesus' feet with half the population of Capernaum looking on! Nicodemus, another teacher, had dared to come to Jesus only by night. Would Jairus lose his position as a synagogue leader? Who would leak the word to his superiors in Jerusalem?

I have the feeling that Jairus cared nothing for the crowd's opinion or for whatever the consequences of his actions might be. Jairus had only one thing on his mind: his daughter's life. There was an almost tangible sense of relief when Jesus started toward Jairus' house. But then Jesus stopped to address a woman who had touched his cloak and been healed. Jesus turned to see who had touched him, commended her faith, and affirmed her healing. There stood Jairus, thinking, "We've got to hurry!" And sure enough, before they started on their way again, a messenger came with the news that the little girl had died. But Jesus said to Jairus, "Don't be afraid; just believe."

Arriving at the home of Jairus, Jesus drove away the wailing mourners, entered with three disciples and the parents, took the dead girl's hand, and said, "Young girl, I tell you to stand up!" And she did. The master of life and death had compassion for a grieving family and gave them back their child. Families form the very core of God's plan for his people. Jesus cares for the families represented by your kids every bit as much as he cared for the family of Jairus.

Colossians 3:12-21

Being a member of a loving family is *work!* While we look to the interests of others, we need to be ready to forgive quickly when our own wants and needs get less than top priority. It's unrealistic to say there should never be spats and hurt feelings, but it's quite realistic to expect loving communication and freely given forgiveness.

UNDERSTANDING YOUR KIDS

Teaching a lesson on families is always tricky because you can't be sure what kinds of family-related trauma your kids may be facing. Single-parent and blended families are nearly as common in the church as in society at large.

Because children tend to blame themselves for whatever goes wrong in their families, it's important for each child to come away from this lesson with the clear understanding that his or her family is important to God, no matter what that family looks like. The Bible is full of stories about imperfect families. Use this lesson to help kids understand that they can serve God by showing respect, love, and care for each member of their families.

The Lesson 😊

ATTENTION GRABBER

Baby Boom

Teacher Tip

Be sure to collect and discard all broken balloon pieces promptly to prevent choking hazards.

As kids arrive, assign them to teams of four, keeping even numbers of younger and older children or adults on each team. If the number of people in your class isn't evenly divisible by four, ask for volunteers to be helpers. Give each team member an uninflated balloon. Place a long strip of masking tape down one side of the room, about five feet from a wall. Have teams stand behind that line. Have helpers place the following items by the wall opposite each team: a large potato, a bowl of water, a bar of soap, two paper towels, and a safety pin.

Say: **We're going to start our lesson on families today with a wild and crazy baby boom relay. When I say "go," blow up and tie off your balloon as quickly as you can. You can help your teammates—it's okay if your "stronger windbags" blow up all the balloons. Once your balloons are tied off, drop them on the floor and "hatch" them by sitting on them and popping them. When your team has hatched all its balloons, you and your teammates will take turns running to the opposite wall to do these four tasks:**

♦ **Use soap, water, and a paper towel to wash and dry the potato "baby."**

♦ **Pin a paper towel "diaper" on the potato baby.**

♦ **Rock the baby and sing one verse of "Jesus Loves Me."**

♦ **Toss the baby back to the rest of the team.**

I'll give you a minute to decide which team member will do each task. You all have to participate. My helpers will make sure you perform each task carefully and completely.

Give teams a few moments to decide which teammate will do each task. Review the directions and assure kids that you'll call out the directions during the game.

When the teams have organized themselves, say "go!" Keep a close watch on each team's progress and be ready to prompt teams on their next task. Helpers can determine if tasks need to be repeated. When all the potato babies have been cared for and tossed to team members behind the line, have kids give themselves a round of applause.

Then say: **Sit in a circle with your teammates and your potato baby and discuss these questions:**

♦ **How was working together in this game like how families work together?** (They have to take turns taking care of little children; families are in a hurry most of the time; caring for babies is hard work.)

♦ **How was it different?** (You wouldn't throw a real baby; in families parents usually do more work than children.)

♦ **What are some things you remember about being a teeny-tiny child?** (I remember a rocking horse; I remember blowing out birthday candles; I remember getting a puppy.)

Call everyone together and invite groups to share what they learned in their discussions.

Say: **It takes lots of work to raise a child. When you were little, your parents had to watch over you constantly. They fed you and changed you in the middle of the night—even when they were so sleepy they could hardly stand up! God puts us in families because he knows that we all need that special love and care that a family gives. Today we're going to learn that ★ Jesus cares about our families.**

BIBLE STUDY

Jairus Visits (Mark 5:21-24, 35-43)

You may want to ask a teenager or adult to visit your classroom in costume as Jairus and tell the story "A Desperate Father" on the next page. Or, if you have parents in your class, ask for a volunteer to slip on a Bible-times costume and read the story.

Say: **I've asked a special visitor to come to our class today and tell us how Jesus helped his family. Let's welcome Jairus!**

Have "Jairus" shake hands with the children and ask their names. Then have him gather everyone in a circle on the floor to hear his story.

After the story, have everyone give Jairus a round of applause. Then ask:

♦ **Do you think it was easy or hard for Jairus to ask Jesus for help?** (Easy, because he was afraid his daughter would die; hard, because he might get in trouble with the other Jewish leaders and lose his job.)

♦ **How did Jairus feel when he had to push through the crowd to get to Jesus?** (Scared that he'd be too late; afraid that Jesus might not come in time.)

♦ **Why did Jesus agree to go with Jairus when he was already talking to a whole crowd of people?** (Because he knew how much Jairus loved his daughter; because Jairus had lots of faith; because he cared about Jairus' family.)

Say: ★ **Jesus cares about our families today, just as he cared for Jairus' family long ago. Let's have some fun discovering more of what the Bible has to say about families.**

A DESPERATE FATHER

(based on Mark 5:21-24, 35-43)

Good morning! When I heard that you were learning that ★ Jesus cares about our families, I just had to visit your class. You see, Jesus did something for my family that I'll never, ever forget.

My name is Jairus, and I'm a leader of the synagogue in the city of Capernaum. A synagogue is like a Jewish church. People come to the synagogue to worship God, pray, listen to the priests, and read from the Scriptures.

When we heard that Jesus was coming to our town, everyone was excited. Well, almost everyone. Some of the Jewish leaders here and in Jerusalem think Jesus is a fake. I don't agree. No one but the Son of God could do the miracles Jesus does! But I've learned to keep quiet about my opinions so that I don't get in trouble.

My story is about my daughter. She's a 12-year-old bundle of energy and laughter and love! One night my wife heard our daughter cry out in her sleep. She got up to see what was wrong, then came running back to me.

"Jairus! Jairus!" she cried, shaking my shoulder. "Our daughter is burning up with fever! I don't know what's wrong—what shall we do?"

We sat by her bed the rest of the night, but there was nothing we could do to help her. By morning she didn't even know who we were. A hard lump of fear knotted in my chest.

"She's going to die, isn't she?" my wife asked.

Just then I heard some of our neighbors out in the street. "Come down to the lake," they shouted to anyone who would listen. "Jesus, the teacher from Nazareth, is there."

"If anyone can help our daughter, Jesus can," I told my wife excitedly. "If I could just get him to come here..."

"Hurry then, Jairus," my wife urged. "Go quickly! You must get him to come before it's too late."

I found Jesus in the middle of a huge crowd of people. "Let me through!" I cried, but everyone wanted to be close to Jesus. I pushed and shoved until I finally got through. Then I fell at Jesus' feet.

"My little daughter is dying! Please come and put your hands on her so that she will be healed and live," I begged.

Jesus agreed to come. "We must hurry!" I urged. But then a woman touched Jesus' cloak and was healed. When Jesus stopped to talk to her, I almost panicked. Then I felt one of my servants tugging at my sleeve.

"Your daughter is dead," he said. "Why bother the teacher anymore?"

Before I could respond, Jesus looked me straight in the eye. "Don't be afraid," he said. "Just believe."

I tried to believe—what else could I do? When we arrived at my house, Jesus asked the mourners, "Why are you crying and making so much noise? The child is not dead, only asleep."

Some people laughed at Jesus, but I kept on praying he was right. He went to the bed where she lay all white and still. He took her hand and commanded, "Young girl, I tell you to stand up!" And she stood up, ran to my wife and me, and gave us a big hug.

Jesus smiled at us as we stood there hugging and crying. He gently reminded us to give our daughter something to eat, and then he left. I'll never forget that day. I learned that Jesus really does care about families, and not only families in Bible times. ★ Jesus cares about your family, too.

Permission to photocopy this handout granted for local church use. Copyright © Lois Keffer.
Published in *All-in-One Sunday School Volume 2* by Group Publishing, Inc., 1515 Cascade Ave., Loveland, CO 80538.

LIFE APPLICATION

Countin' on You!

Have kids rejoin their groups of four. Have the extra people who were helpers during the Attention Grabber join other groups—it's okay to have groups of different sizes.

Say: **In your group, decide who will be the mom, who will be the dad, who will be a big kid, and who will be a little kid. It's okay to have more than one big kid or little kid.**

While groups are assigning their roles, set on a table sandwich bags; several tablespoons; and bowls of dried cranberries, M&M's, and raisins.

Say: **When I call out "dads," I want all the dads to pop up and take turns telling what families count on dads to do. When you've named all the things you can think of, I'll tell you what to do next. Then we'll repeat the game with all the other family members. When we're finished, you'll have a delicious treat to enjoy. Here we go. Dads!**

Have all the dads pop up and take turns telling what families count on dads to do. Kids might mention taking care of the car, mowing the lawn, cooking on the grill, bringing home a paycheck, talking through problems, or helping with schoolwork.

After the dads have named all the responsibilities they can think of, say: **OK, dads, run to the table and take a sandwich bag to everyone in your group.**

Then call out "moms." Kids may mention planning birthday parties, getting groceries, planning meals, bringing home a paycheck, taking care of people when they're sick, tucking children in at night, or taking kids to music lessons. When kids have named all the responsibilities they can think of, have the moms run back and forth between the table and their groups, putting a spoonful of raisins in each person's bag.

Next call out, "big kids." Kids may mention taking out the garbage, feeding the pets, helping with dishes, mowing the lawn, baby-sitting, or running errands. When kids have named all the responsibilities they can think of, have the big kids run back and forth between the table and their groups, putting a spoonful of dried cereal in each person's bag.

Finally call out, "little kids." Kids may mention such things as giving hugs, telling jokes, bringing joy and laughter, picking up toys, and obeying parents. When kids have named all the things they can think of, have the little kids run back and forth between the table and their groups, putting a spoonful of M&M's in each person's bag.

Encourage kids to enjoy their treats as they discuss these questions in their groups:

♦ **What did we gain by working together as a family in this activity?** (We got a good treat; food!)

Teacher Tip

Be open to all of the suggestions, even if they don't conform to traditional roles.

♦ **What do we gain by working together in our real families?** (A happy home; good feelings; love for each other.)

♦ **Why do you think God put us in families?** (So we can care for each other; so we'll have people who love us.)

Invite kids to share what they learned from their discussions.

Then say: **In families, we count on each other for lots of things. And that's why God put us in families. Not all families look alike, so sometimes we count on each other for different things. Listen to what the Bible says about how important it is to take care of each other in our families.** Have a volunteer look up and read 1 Timothy 5:8.

Say: **The Bible tells us that taking care of each other in our families is one of the most important things we can do. God put us in families so we would have people to love us and take care of us. That's why ★ Jesus cares about our families.**

COMMITMENT

Thanks to You!

Say: **When you put people together under the same roof day after day and year after year, things won't always be perfect! We all get the crabbies and grouchies, and when we do, the other people in our families had better watch out! Let's find out more about what the Bible says people should do to build loving, happy families.**

Distribute Bibles to each group. Assign half of the groups Colossians 3:12-14. Assign the other groups Colossians 3:15-21. Have groups search their passages for God's instructions for families. Allow two or three minutes for study, and then call everyone together and ask groups to report what they discovered.

Say: **Turn to a partner and discuss these questions:**

♦ **Which of these instructions is hardest for you to follow?** (Obeying parents; being thankful when things aren't going well.)

♦ **What can you do to get better at it?** (Ask God to remind me; think of others instead of just thinking of myself.)

Say: **I know there's one thing we can all do better. When we count on people for the same thing day after day, it's easy to forget to say thank you. So today we're going to take time to make thank you notes for the people in our families.**

Set out scissors, markers or colored pencils, and photocopies of the "From the Bottom of My Heart" and "Thanks a Bunch" handouts. Encourage kids to make cards for people in their families who would appreciate a special thank you. Have kids decorate their cards and fill in the names of the people who'll receive them. Then demonstrate how to fold and cut each card.

1. Cut around the border of each card.

2. Fold each card in half the long way.

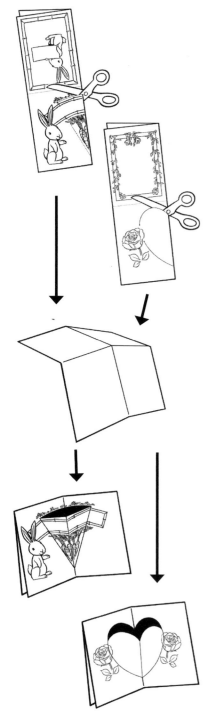

3. Cut the heart from the top center to the upper dots; then cut from the bottom center to the lower dots.

4. Cut the "Thanks a Bunch" banner from the top center to the upper dots and from the dot below the carrots to the banner.

5. Fold each card in half the other way.

6. Pull the center of each card forward and fold it as you close the card so the design will pop up when the card is opened.

As kids create their cards, circulate and ask questions such as "What's one really happy time you remember sharing with your family?" and "What do you like best about your family?"

As time for working on the cards draws to a close, give two-minute and one-minute warnings. Then gather everyone for the closing activity.

Teacher Tip

You may want to provide extra handouts for kids to take home so they can make a card for everyone in their families.

CLOSING

Circles of Love

Have kids set their cards aside and then stand in circles in their groups of four and hold hands. If you've invited parents for today's lesson, have families stand together in a circle.

Say: **Listen and follow my instructions carefully.** Give these instructions in a spirit of quiet reflection, pausing for a moment after each one.

♦ **If you've ever failed to say thank you when someone in your family did something nice for you, drop your hands and close your eyes.**

♦ **If you've ever lost your temper and shouted at a family member, turn around and face away from your circle.**

♦ **If you've ever complained to an outsider about someone in your family, take a step away from your circle.**

♦ **If you've ever hurt the feelings of someone in your family, take another step away.**

♦ **If you've ever tried to encourage someone in your family, turn around.**

♦ **If you've ever helped take care of a family member who was sick, take a step toward your circle.**

♦ **If you've ever given up your plans to do what another family member wanted to do, take another step toward your circle.**

♦ **If you've ever forgiven a family member who hurt your feelings, open your eyes and put your arms around the people on either side of you.**

Say: **Please remain in your circles as I close in prayer.**

Pray: **Dear Lord, thank you for caring about our families. Remind us this week to show love and appreciation to each member of our families. Help us to be slow to get angry and quick to forgive. In Jesus' name, amen.**

from the bottom of my heart!

THANKS

DEAR

_____

For all the things

you do each day,

It makes me very

glad to say...

Permission to photocopy this handout granted for local church use.
Copyright © Lois Keffer. Published in *All-in-One Sunday School Volume 2* by
Group Publishing, Inc., 1515 Cascade Ave., Loveland, CO 80538.

Thanks a Bunch!

YOU'RE
the world's
BEST

I have a hunch,
So I want to say...

Permission to photocopy this handout granted for local church use.
Copyright © Lois Keffer. Published in *All-in-One Sunday School Volume 2* by
Group Publishing, Inc., 1515 Cascade Ave., Loveland, CO 80538.

LESSON 9

LESSON AIM

To help kids understand that ★ Jesus helps us when we're discouraged.

Teacher Tip

This lesson works well with an intergenerational class. You may wish to invite whole families to join you for this session.

OBJECTIVES

Kids or families will

✓ brainstorm situations in which they feel discouraged,
✓ learn that the risen Jesus helped his discouraged disciples,
✓ discover that Jesus always has the power to help, and
✓ commit to trusting God in every situation.

YOU'LL NEED

❏ a rope
❏ fish-shaped crackers*
❏ a Bible
❏ markers
❏ scissors
❏ transparent tape
❏ newsprint
❏ balloons
❏ photocopies of the "Sailing Through Discouragement" handout (p. 97)
❏ photocopies of the "Folded Fish-Basket" handout (p. 98)
Always check for allergies before serving snacks.

BIBLE BASIS

John 21:1-14

In Jesus' third post-resurrection appearance to a group of his disciples, he appeared on the shore of the Sea of Galilee after several of the disciples had spent a long night fishing without success. The disciples saw a stranger on the shore who advised them to cast their nets on the right side of the boat. When the weary disciples accommodated the stranger, their net immediately bulged with a catch so large they couldn't haul it back into the boat. Taking a closer look at the helpful stranger, John said, "It is the Lord!" After struggling to bring their boat and miraculous catch of fish to shore, the disciples found that Jesus had made a fire and prepared a welcome breakfast of warm bread and grilled fish.

I'm always intrigued by the fact that the disciples made that one last toss of the net. Had I been in the boat, I probably would have sneered, "Yeah, right!" and rowed away. Jesus always helps us, but always in his time, in his way, and often after a great deal of effort on our part. Compare a night of fruitless fishing to a math concept that can't be conquered, an enemy who won't become a friend, or a hoped-for job that just doesn't materialize. Perseverance and faith are the qualities God nurtures in us as we hang on and keep trying, believing that God will make all things beautiful in his time.

Ephesians 4:29

Have you ever noticed how certain individuals generate a strong "personal atmosphere"? Some people radiate enthusiasm, good humor, sympathy, or a sense of calm. Others reflect pessimism, skepticism, or tension. This Scripture challenges us to be encouragers—positive people who consciously do and say what will build up others in the body of Christ.

UNDERSTANDING YOUR KIDS

How many times have you seen an art project that started with enthusiasm but ended up crumpled in a wastebasket? a hiker who couldn't wait to start up the trail but before long wanted to give up and turn back? a new school year marked by fresh determination that soured by the end of September? a long-saved-for purchase given up in favor of a lesser item that granted more immediate gratification? Ah, the frustrations of childhood!

Children lack the benefit of experience and the perspective it offers. That's why adults who are willing to offer help and encouragement are so crucial to kids' early successes. What a difference one compassionate, caring adult can make to a child who feels utterly hopeless when faced with taking a math test, making friends in a new place, or performing in a recital. As a teacher, that's just the kind of difference you're making in kids' lives each week. Congratulations and bless you! Children who've learned that they can count on help and encouragement from adults find it easy to put that same kind of trust in God. Use this lesson to help kids understand that Jesus is always there for them, and that unlike ordinary encouragers, he has unlimited power to help.

The Lesson 😊

ATTENTION GRABBER

Poor Kitty

As kids arrive, have them help you place chairs in a circle. You'll need one less chair than there are people in class.

Say: **We're going to begin today with a really funny game called Poor Kitty. The person who's "It" has to kneel in front of someone who's sitting in a chair and meow. The person in the chair has to keep a perfectly straight face; pat It on the head; and say, "Poor Kitty." If the person in the chair cracks a smile or laughs, he or she is It. If the person doesn't smile, It goes to someone else and meows.**

Choose someone who's funny and outgoing to be It first. It may purr, make funny faces, meow several times, or rub his or her head on a player's knee. If you have time, play until everyone has had a chance to be It. Give a round of applause to the people who best resisted the impulse to smile. Then ask:

♦ **In real life, what makes you laugh and smile?** (Jokes; when something good happens; when I see something funny on TV.)

♦ **When is it hard to make people smile?** (When bad things happen; when they're sick or tired.)

Say: **Turn to a partner and tell about a time you were really discouraged and didn't smile much at all.** Allow a couple of minutes for partners to share.

Then say: **Our Bible story today is about a bunch of really discouraged fishermen. Raise your hand if you've ever gone fishing and gotten discouraged.** Pause to let kids briefly share their experiences. **The fishermen we're going to hear about just happened to be Jesus' disciples. They discovered in quite a unique way that ★ Jesus helps us when we're discouraged.**

BIBLE STUDY

What a Catch! (John 21:1-14)

Say: **To get ready for our story, we need a fishing boat, a big net, fishermen, and some fish.**

Using a length of rope, have kids help you outline the shape of a boat in the middle of the floor. The outline should be large enough to hold several kids. Recruit a third of your kids to be the "fishermen," Jesus' disciples. Have the fishermen stand near the boat. Have another third of your kids be the "net." Instruct that group to join hands and sit on the floor near the boat. Have the remaining kids be the "fish" and huddle on the opposite side of the boat from the net.

When everyone is in place, say: **We need to do one more thing before we begin the story. Fish and net groups, your part goes like this: "Ain't no fish, ain't no fish, ain't no fish here in this sea."** Have the fish and net groups use a rap beat and lots of enthusiasm as they repeat their line.

Fishermen, your part goes like this: "Baaad luck, baaad luck, sure seems like bad luck to me." Have the fishermen repeat their line. **Listen carefully and act out your part in the story. When I point to you, be ready to say your line. Here we go!**

One night, not long after Jesus had been crucified, a somber Peter said, "I'm going out to fish." Several other disciples said, "We'll go, too." So they all got aboard their fishing boat. Cue the fishermen to get into the boat. **They pulled a big net into the boat, too, because they planned to catch a lot of fish.** Signal the fishermen to "pull" the net group into the boat.

At 11 o'clock, they threw their net into the water. Signal the net group to jump out of the boat. **But when they dragged the net back toward the boat, it was empty.**

Signal the net group to jump into the boat and then shout along with the fish, "Ain't no fish, ain't no fish, ain't no fish here in this sea." Have the fishermen shake their heads and say, "Baaad luck, baaad luck, sure seems like bad luck to me."

At midnight, the fishermen threw their net into the water again. Signal the net group to jump out of the boat. **But when they dragged the net back toward the boat, it was empty.** Signal the net group to jump into the boat. Have the fish and net groups repeat their line; then have the fishermen repeat theirs.

Repeat this sequence for 1 o'clock, 2 o'clock, 3 o'clock, 4 o'clock, and 5 o'clock.

At 6 o'clock the fishermen were tired and discouraged. But then a stranger hailed them from the shore. "Friends," he called, "have you caught any fish?"

"No!" the discouraged fishermen called back.

"Throw your net on the other side of the boat!" the stranger shouted.

So the fishermen tossed the net on the other side of the boat. Have the net group scamper into the boat and then jump out the other side. **Suddenly the net bulged with fish!** Have the fish group "swim" over and jump into the net.

Say: **Fish and net, say, "Check out the fish, check out the fish, check out the fish here in this sea!"** Pause for the fish and net groups to say their new line. **Fishermen, say, "Goood luck, goood luck, sure seems like good luck to me."** Pause for the fishermen to say their line.

The net was so full of fish that the fishermen couldn't even pull it back into the boat. Have the fishermen struggle to "pull" the net and fish, and then give up. **Then one of the fishermen pointed**

at the stranger on the shore. "That's no stranger," he shouted excitedly. "It's the Lord!"

Sure enough, it was Jesus. And he had built a fire and had a hot, tasty breakfast ready for his tired, hungry disciples. And I have a tasty treat ready for you for doing such a good job with the Bible story.

Pour fish-shaped crackers into each child's cupped hands. Have the fishermen, net, and fish groups form separate circles and discuss these questions.

♦ **What do you think the disciples thought after fishing all night and catching nothing?** (They were tired; discouraged.)

♦ **If you had been in that boat, would you have wanted to toss the net out once more? Why or why not?** (Yes, because I don't like to give up; no, because I would've been sick of trying.)

♦ **Why do you think Jesus helped his disciples make this miraculous catch of fish?** (So they would still have faith in his power; because he loved them and didn't want them to be discouraged.)

Say: ★ **Jesus helps us when we're discouraged, just as he helped his disciples long ago. Let's find out what's discouraging to you and how Jesus can help us get through discouraging times.**

LIFE APPLICATION

Balloon Fish

Have kids remain in their three groups. Give each group markers, scissors, transparent tape, and a sheet of newsprint. Give a balloon to each child. Have kids blow up and tie off their balloons and then draw fish faces on them.

Say: **Now set your balloon fish behind you for a moment. Choose a recorder for your group—someone who can write quickly. You'll also need a Bible reader and a reporter.** Pause for groups to choose people for those roles. **In just a moment I'll ask you to brainstorm with your group all the discouraging things you can think of—things such as getting the measles or getting cut from a team. At the end of two minutes, we'll share our lists of discouragements. Go!**

After two minutes, ask reporters to share their groups' lists.

Say: **Wow! That was terrible to listen to. I think we should stop and sob for a few seconds.** Lead the group in making loud sobbing sounds. **That's better. Now take your fish balloon and a marker. Write on your fish the three things you heard that would be the most discouraging to you. You may write things that have actually happened to you or things you hope never will happen to you. Some of you may need to help the younger kids write on their balloons. After you've all written on your balloons, tell your**

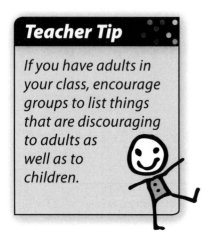

Teacher Tip

If you have adults in your class, encourage groups to list things that are discouraging to adults as well as to children.

group what you wrote and why.

Allow three or four minutes for sharing. Then say: **Enough of this doom and gloom! Now it's time to hear the good news straight from the Bible.**

Distribute photocopies of the "Sailing Through Discouragement" handout. Have the readers in each group read aloud the three verses on the handout.

Then say: **These promises from the Bible can help us sail right through discouraging times. You'll notice that these verses are printed on fish tails and fins. I'd like you to cut them out and carefully tape them to your balloon fish. They'll help you remember that ★ Jesus helps us when we're discouraged.**

Demonstrate how to cut through the × in the fish tail and slip the tied end of the balloon through the cut. Kids may want to curl the strips of the tail and fin pieces around a pencil. Then show kids how to use tape to attach the fins.

Say: **It's great to know that ★ Jesus helps us when we're discouraged. We can count on other people in God's family to encourage us, too. Let's see how that works.**

Have kids hold their balloons and form a circle. Say: **When I call out "fish," toss your balloons in the air if you were in that group. Then all of us will make sure those balloons stay in the air. We'll keep bopping them and try not to let any balloons fall to the ground. When I call out "nets," the members of that group will toss their balloons in the air. Finally I'll call out "fishermen," and the fishermen will toss their balloons in the air. Remember: We want to keep all the balloons in the air, so bee-bop-balloon-bop for all you're worth!**

Call out "fish," then "nets," then "fishermen" at 15-second intervals. Keep the balloon bop going for about a minute and a half. Then call time and have kids retrieve their own balloons, sit down, and take three deep breaths. Have a volunteer read Ephesians 4:29. Then ask:

♦ **What does this Bible verse tell us to do?** (Encourage each other; build each other up.)

♦ **Why do you think it's important to do that in God's family?** (Because we need each other; because God wants us to love each other as much as we love ourselves.)

♦ **How was what we did in this game like what this Bible verse tells us to do?** (We helped each other stay "up"; we tried to keep each other's balloons from falling.)

Say: **It's great to have brothers and sisters in Christ who we can count on to encourage us. It doesn't matter if you're older or younger or somewhere in the middle; a kind word of encouragement from you can really help someone get through a tough time. Let's have fun making an encouraging gift.**

Teacher Tip

You may want to photocopy the "Sailing Through Discouragement" handout on neon yellow or orange paper. If you use white paper, encourage students to use colored pencils or markers to add colorful swirls or gradations of color to the fins and tails before they add them to the balloon fish.

Teacher Tip

Be sure to collect and discard all broken balloon pieces promptly to prevent choking hazards.

COMMITMENT

A Basket of Encouragement

Before class make a sample fish basket from the "Folded Fish-Basket" handout to show the kids.

Have kids re-form their three groups. Distribute photocopies of the handout. Display your finished basket, and then help kids cut out and fold their own. You'll enjoy the "oohs" and "ahs" when kids discover that pulling on the pointed ends of the folded pattern makes a basket suddenly appear!

Circulate among kids as they work. Pour fish-shaped crackers into the baskets as kids complete them. Ask:

♦ **How do you think a cheerful heart can be like good medicine?** (A happy outlook makes me feel better; smiles help, no matter what goes wrong.)

♦ **Why do you think God wants us to depend on him when we're discouraged?** (Because he knows the bigger plan; because it keeps me close to him.)

♦ **What does it mean to you that God is on your side?** (That I don't need to be afraid; that God will help me; that things will turn out for the best.)

♦ **How will the fish-shaped crackers in your basket remind you that ★ Jesus helps us when we're discouraged?** (I'll remember how he helped the disciples after their long night of fishing; I'll remember that Jesus can do anything and that he loves me just as he loved his disciples.)

Say: ★ **Jesus helps us when we're discouraged. Sometimes we find encouragement in God's Word, as with the verses printed on your baskets. Sometimes we find encouragement in prayer or in the way God makes things happen. And sometimes we find encouragement in each other.**

CLOSING

Baskets of Prayer

Have kids gather in a circle with their completed baskets. Say: **Let's be silent for a moment. I'd like you to decide if you're going to keep your basket because you need encouragement or if you're going to give it away. Then I'll close with a prayer.**

Pause for a few moments. Then pray: **Dear Jesus, thank you for the many ways ★ you help us when we're discouraged. Help us to have cheerful hearts and to encourage each other, too. Amen.**

Remind kids to take their baskets and balloon fish with them. You may want to set out extra "Folded Fish-Basket" handouts for kids who want to make extra baskets to give away.

Teacher Tip

Teach a helper or two how to make the fish basket before the rest of the students arrive. Then your helpers can coach other students who feel hesitant about doing origami.

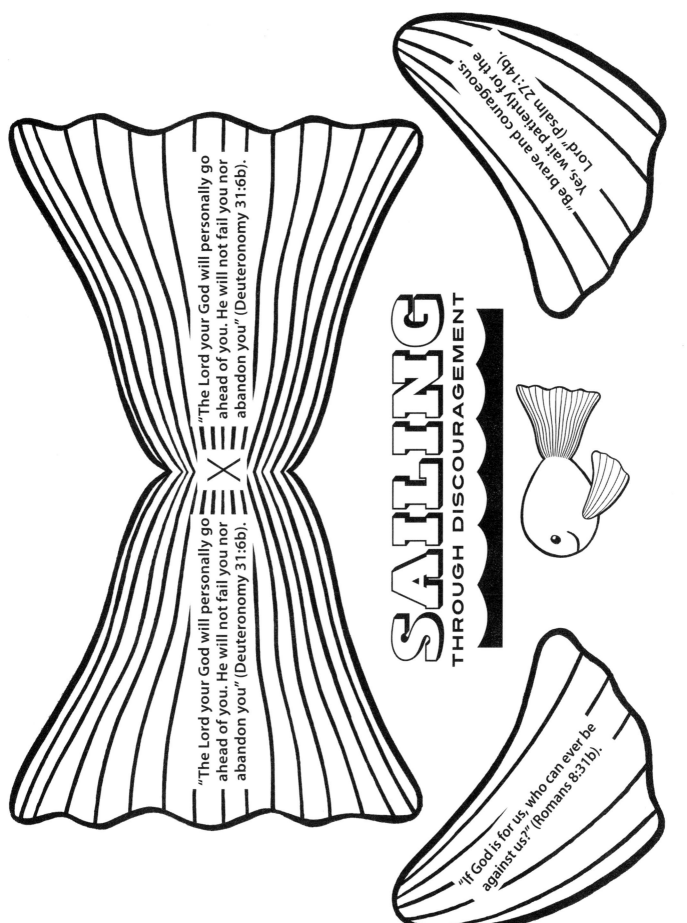

"The Lord your God will personally go ahead of you. He will not fail you nor abandon you" (Deuteronomy 31:6b).

"The Lord your God will personally go ahead of you. He will not fail you nor abandon you" (Deuteronomy 31:6b).

SAILING
THROUGH DISCOURAGEMENT

"Be brave and courageous. Yes, wait patiently for the Lord" (Psalm 27:14b).

"If God is for us, who can ever be against us?" (Romans 8:31b).

Permission to photocopy this handout granted for local church use. Copyright © Lois Keffer. Published in *All-in-One Sunday School Volume 2* by Group Publishing, Inc., 1515 Cascade Ave., Loveland, CO 80538.

FOLDED FISH BASKET

1. Cut out the fish basket on the heavy lines. With the pattern facing you, fold it in half the long way; then open.

2. Fold forward from A to B; then open.

3. Fold forward from C to D; then open.

4. Fold the pattern in half backward between the two small hearts; then open.

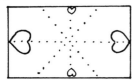

5. Push the two small hearts together; then push the two large hearts together.

6. Fold the two bottom corners to the middle, creating a diamond. Turn the pattern over and repeat.

7. Fold both side points to the center. Turn the pattern over and repeat.

8. Fold the pattern in half both ways to crease.

9. Gently pull the points of the open end apart to form a box with flaps.

10. Crease the bottom edges of the box to flatten the bottom and fill the box with fish-shaped crackers.

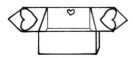

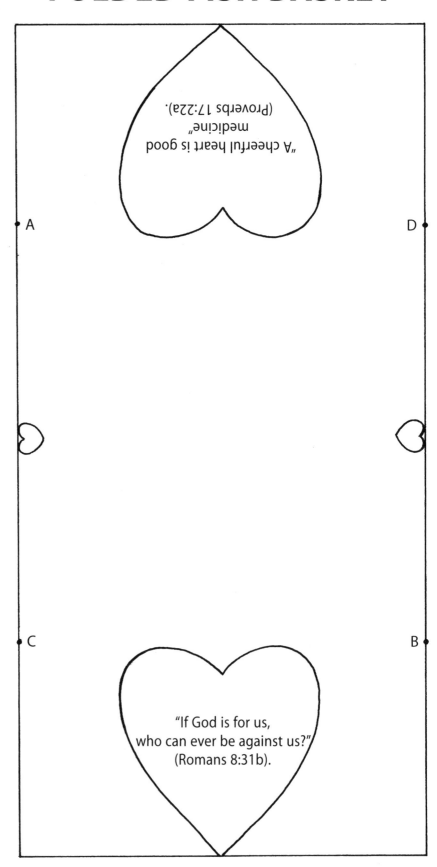

"A cheerful heart is good medicine" (Proverbs 17:22a).

"If God is for us, who can ever be against us?" (Romans 8:31b).

A   D

C   B

Permission to photocopy this handout granted for local church use. Copyright © Lois Keffer.
Published in *All-in-One Sunday School Volume 2* by Group Publishing, Inc., 1515 Cascade Ave., Loveland, CO 80538.

LESSON AIM

To help kids understand that ★ we forgive as God forgives us.

OBJECTIVES

Kids will

✓ experience grace by getting prizes without earning them,
✓ act out the story of the lost son receiving forgiveness from his father,
✓ name things for which they have been forgiven, and
✓ be willing to pass on forgiveness to others.

YOU'LL NEED

❏ six 2-liter bottles
❏ several plastic holders from six-packs of soft drinks
❏ scissors
❏ masking tape
❏ 3 nickels per child
❏ paper
❏ pencils
❏ Bibles
❏ photocopies of the "Forgiveness Is a Two-Way Street" hand-out (p. 105)
❏ ribbon

You'll also need three grocery bags with the following items in them:

❏ grocery bag 1: a 3×5 card with Luke 15:11-14 written on it, a stack of play money, and a backpack;
❏ grocery bag 2: a 3×5 card with Luke 15:15-20 written on it, a dirty work shirt, and a plastic container with food scraps in it; and
❏ grocery bag 3: a 3×5 card with Luke 15:21-24 written on it, a bathrobe, a pair of men's sandals, and a ring made of aluminum foil.

all-in-one
SUNDAY
SCHOOL

BIBLE BASIS

Luke 15:11-32

The parable of the prodigal son illustrates forgiveness at its best—and worst. The irresponsible young man who stars in this story did things that were unthinkable in a family of that day. He took his inheritance before his father's death; he blew the money on selfish, wild living; and then proceeded to live the lowest life as a pig farmer. Yet, in spite of it all, the father freely offered forgiveness and acceptance when the repentant son found his way home. God still offers that same unconditional forgiveness to anyone who will "come home" to him today.

Matthew 6:14-15

Because God so freely forgives us, we in turn are to forgive others. The concept of forgiving so we can be forgiven isn't terribly comfortable for kids or adults. We want to be forgiven, and then—like the older brother in the story—decide for ourselves whether others deserve our forgiveness. Jesus' challenge reminds us forgiving others isn't optional—it's part of his call to discipleship.

UNDERSTANDING YOUR KIDS

It's been said that when it comes to forgiveness, kids ought to be teaching adults. One of the world's most amazing sights is two best buddies walking side by side after a shouting match just moments before. Long-lasting grudges and feuds seldom develop among children unless the conflict is fueled by adults. This lesson capitalizes on the forgiving nature of the younger generation, and on kids' sincere desire for simple, harmonious relationships.

This forgiving nature is balanced by a strong sense of justice, especially in older kids. They, like the older brother in the prodigal son story, want to see "bad guys" get what they've got coming. The challenge here is to help kids see we're all sinners adopted into God's family by his grace. This grace is free to anyone, any time. And since God freely gives it to us, he expects us to pass it on to others.

Secular culture gives kids a strong message—revenge and paybacks feel good. We need to show them forgiveness feels better.

ATTENTION GRABBER

No-Loss Toss

Set up a ringtoss game with six 2-liter bottles arranged in a triangle like bowling pins. Cut apart several plastic rings that hold six-packs of soft drinks together. Kids will try to toss the rings over the necks of the bottles.

Use masking tape to mark a "toss line" for younger kids about 3 feet back from the bottles. Mark a second line a couple of feet farther away for older kids.

Say: **We're going to play a ringtoss game. For every ring you land over the neck of a bottle, I'll give you a nickel.**

Give kids each three tries, and award a nickel for each try whether the ring lands on a bottle or not. If kids are puzzled by your generosity, just ignore them and keep the game going. Have the group cheer for the efforts of every player.

After the game, ask:

♦ **What do you think was different about this game?** (We kept getting nickels whether we earned them or not.)

♦ **How did you feel about getting nickels when you messed up and didn't really earn them?** (Like I didn't deserve them; I thought it was great.)

Ask the kids who actually landed the rings on the bottles:

♦ **How did you feel when you landed the rings but ended up getting the same prize as people who didn't land any?** (It made me mad because I earned a prize and the others didn't; I felt kind of cheated.)

♦ **How is getting a prize when you didn't earn it like getting forgiveness when you mess up in real life?** (I don't really deserve what I'm getting.)

Say: **The amazing and wonderful thing is that no matter how many times we mess up in life, God is always willing to give us his free gift of forgiveness. With God, it doesn't matter if we're winners or losers, or how many times we've blown it. He offers us forgiveness if we ask for it, no matter what. ★ And he wants us to forgive as he forgives us.**

Today we're going to participate in a story Jesus told about somebody who messed up big time. In fact, there wasn't a whole lot more he could have done wrong. Let's see how things turned out for him.

BIBLE STUDY

A Father Forgives (Luke 15:11-32)

Give kids each a sheet of paper and a pencil. Say: **To set the stage for our Bible study, I want you to create an imaginary bedroom for yourself, and you can have anything in it you want. You've got two minutes to draw or write what you'd want in your room. Go!**

Call time after two minutes. Then have kids find partners. Encourage older kids to pair up with younger ones.

Say: **You now have one minute to find out what your partner put in his or her room. Then I'm going to ask each of you to tell about your partner's room.**

Bring everyone together for the pair-share. After kids have told about their partners' ideal rooms, ask:

♦ **What did you think about creating your own room?** (Awesome; I wish I could really have a room like this.)

♦ **Do you think having a room like that would make you happier than anything else? Why or why not?** (Sure, it would be great to have all that stuff; not really, things can't give me love no matter how neat they are.)

Say: **Our story today is about a kid who had it all. He had the best room a Bible-times kid could have. He had a neat family, and his dad was a wealthy landowner. But all this wasn't enough.**

That's all I'm going to tell you of the story. The rest is up to you. Let's form three groups to tell the rest of the story. I have a bag of things for each group to use. In your groups, read your Scripture and then decide how to use the things in your bag to tell the story to the rest of the class.

Give groups each one grocery bag containing the following items:

Group 1: a 3×5 card with Luke 15:11-14 written on it, a stack of play money, and a backpack.

Group 2: a 3×5 card with Luke 15:15-20 written on it, a dirty work shirt, and a plastic container with food scraps in it.

Group 3: a 3×5 card with Luke 15:21-24 written on it, a bathrobe, a pair of men's sandals, and a ring made of aluminum foil.

Allow about three minutes for Bible study and planning; then have groups present their portions of the Bible story.

After the presentations, ask:

♦ **How did it feel to take off with all that money in your hands?** (Cool; I know just how I'd spend it.)

♦ **How did it feel to put on the dirty shirt and smell the food scraps?** (Yucky; I'd never do that.)

♦ **How did it feel to be welcomed home with a big hug and new clothes?** (Weird at first, but then really good.)

♦ **How were those feelings like feelings you've had when someone has forgiven you?** Encourage kids to share their personal

Teacher Tip

If you have older kids who can take the lead in creating skits to tell the story, encourage them to do so. An alternate approach is to let kids act out the story as you read it straight from the Bible.

Teacher Tip

Encourage kids to add lots of sound effects. (They'll love making pig noises!) Don't be afraid to let kids' creativity flow—you can easily refocus the class by using a prearranged attention-getting signal such as flashing the lights or having kids raise their hands in response to your raised hand.

experiences. You might begin by telling about a time when you received forgiveness.

Then say: **Guess what? That isn't the end of the story.**
Read aloud Luke 15:25-32.
Ask:

♦ **Why do you think the older brother was angry?** (Because he stayed home and worked hard, but his younger brother was getting all the attention.)

♦ **Do you think the older brother had a right to feel that way? Why or why not?** (Yes, the younger brother didn't deserve a party; no, the father loved both his sons, but was especially glad to have the younger one home again.)

♦ **How is the father giving a party for his long-lost son similar to how God treats people who ask him for forgiveness?** (No matter how much people sin and mess up their lives, God is always ready to forgive them.)

Say: **Sometimes we might think—like the older brother did—that a person doesn't deserve to be forgiven. But God wants us to always be loving and forgiving, just like he is. ★ God wants us to forgive as he forgives us. Let's look at a Bible verse that explains how God's forgiveness works.**

LIFE APPLICATION

Both Sides of the Street

Give kids each a photocopy of the "Forgiveness Is a Two-Way Street" handout and a pencil.

Have a volunteer read aloud Matthew 6:14-15 from the handout.
Ask:

♦ **How important is it to forgive others?** (Pretty important; God says he won't forgive us unless we do.)

♦ **How is forgiveness like a two-way street?** (It goes both ways—we receive it and give it.)

Say: **On one side of the street, draw or write things God has forgiven you for. On the other side, draw or write things you may need to forgive others for.**

After kids have finished, ask:

♦ **How does it feel to look at the list of things God has forgiven you for?** (It makes me feel glad that God is so loving; it makes me wish I hadn't blown it so often.)

♦ **How does it feel to look at the list of things you need to forgive other people for?** (Angry; I think it will be hard to do.)

♦ **Does seeing the two lists side by side make it easier to forgive others? Why or why not?** (No, I still feel mad when people are mean to me; yes, I realize if God can forgive me for all those things, then I can forgive others.)

Teacher Tip

Younger children may need prompting to get started with this activity. They could draw an angry, shouting face to show how they yelled at someone. On the other side of the street, they could draw a sad face to show that someone said mean things to them, or they could draw a toy that someone broke. Another approach to this activity is to have kids return to the pairs they formed earlier and let older partners act as scribes for younger partners.

COMMITMENT

A Gift From God

Form pairs. Give kids each a 2-foot length of ribbon. Have kids each fold up their handout and wrap it with their ribbon. Have partners work together to tie bows.

Say: **This little package is to remind you forgiveness is a gift from God—a gift he wants you to pass on to others. ★ God wants us to forgive as he forgives us.**

Encourage kids to show their gifts to their parents and to discuss what they wrote or drew.

CLOSING

Forgiveness Circle

Form circles of about eight and join a circle yourself. Have kids stand close together with their arms extended forward and hands with palms up, touching in the center, as if they're about to receive a large gift. Older kids and adults may need to kneel to touch hands with younger children. Pray a simple prayer, thanking God for the gift of forgiveness and asking for his help in passing it on to others.

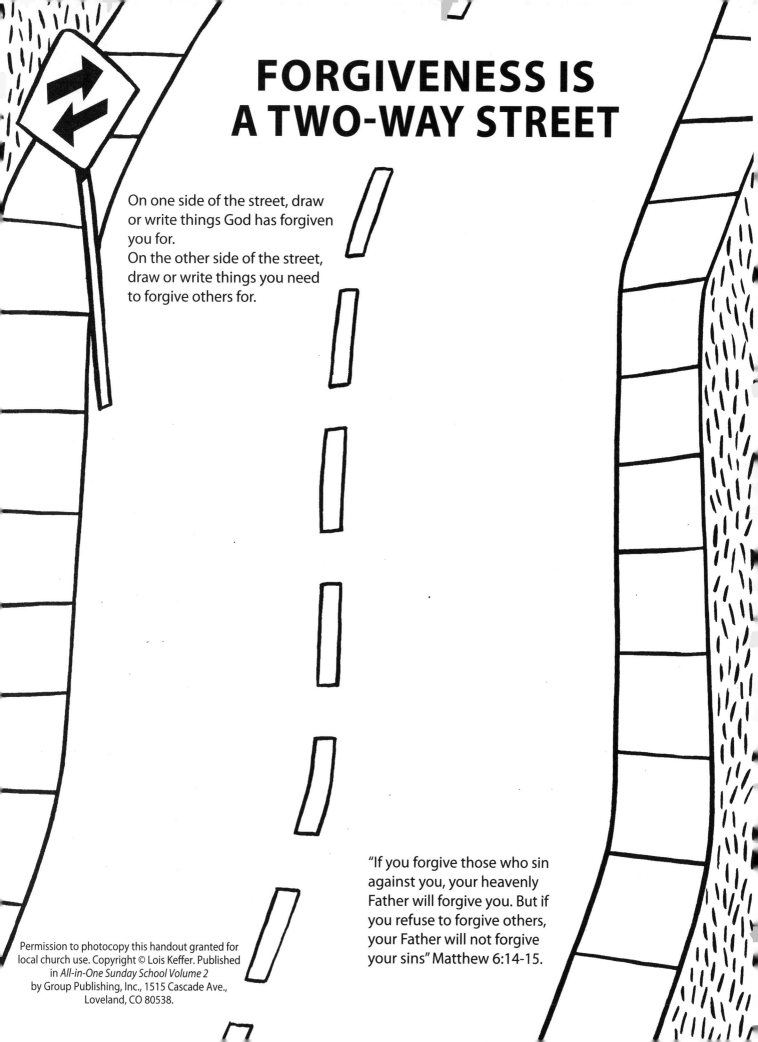

FORGIVENESS IS A TWO-WAY STREET

On one side of the street, draw or write things God has forgiven you for.

On the other side of the street, draw or write things you need to forgive others for.

"If you forgive those who sin against you, your heavenly Father will forgive you. But if you refuse to forgive others, your Father will not forgive your sins" Matthew 6:14-15.

Permission to photocopy this handout granted for local church use. Copyright © Lois Keffer. Published in *All-in-One Sunday School Volume 2* by Group Publishing, Inc., 1515 Cascade Ave., Loveland, CO 80538.

LESSON

11

LESSON AIM

To help kids understand that ★ God wants us to be kind and loving.

Teacher Tip

This lesson works well with an intergenerational class. You may wish to invite whole families to join you for this session.

OBJECTIVES

Kids or families will

✓ discover how it feels to depend on others,

✓ hear Naomi's story,

✓ make gifts of kindness and examine practical ways to show God's love, and

✓ commit to showing kindness to others.

YOU'LL NEED

❏ star stickers
❏ blindfolds
❏ a box of doughnuts*
❏ an adult to play the role of Naomi (optional)
❏ a robe for a Bible-times costume
❏ scissors
❏ markers
❏ tape
❏ photocopies of the "Hearts of Kindness" handout (p. 114)
❏ photocopies of the "Someone Cares Pop-Up Card" handout (p. 115)
❏ glue sticks
❏ a photocopy of the "Love and Kindness Mix" instructions (p. 112)
❏ ingredients for the mix*
❏ a Bible

Always check for allergies before serving snacks.

BIBLE BASIS

Ruth 1–4

The book of Ruth is a wonderful story of selflessness and generosity. It's so beautifully and concisely written that you could practically read the whole book aloud to your class. Read it again yourself and be inspired by God's love interpreted in simple acts of kindness.

The story of Ruth shows us that God can use everyday people to accomplish great things in his kingdom. Ruth was a Moabite, not a Jew. Yet because of her devotion to a sad old woman, Ruth became an ancestress of King David and of Jesus.

Ruth gave up everything that was familiar to her to accompany Naomi back to Bethlehem. She trusted herself to the living God who honored her sacrifice and blessed her greatly in return.

Proverbs 14:21, 31

It has been said that kindness is the language of love. Those who make it a point to be kind are God's everyday heroes. Acts of kindness done in the name of Christ are the building blocks of the kingdom of God. And no one has to wait to be old enough to participate.

UNDERSTANDING YOUR KIDS

Kids are preoccupied with many things. Kindness isn't usually one of them. Kids understand the value of being popular or good at sports or being identified with the right group of friends. But only a few kids recognize the importance of being kind to everyone, regardless of circumstance.

A classic example is what happens in school lunchrooms. Suppose a group of friends squeezes around one table, but one child is left out and has to sit alone. How many of the kids in your class would leave the group to sit with the one who is left out? We hope that some would. But most would probably think, "Whew—I'm glad I'm not the one stuck at the other table!"

Use this lesson to help kids see that God wants us to make kindness a priority—and that he blesses us in surprising ways when we do.

The Lesson 😊

ATTENTION GRABBER

Help Me! Help Me!

Place star stickers on kids (and adults) as they arrive. Put a sticker on the shoe of the first person, on the cheek of the second person, and on the hand of the third person. Continue in this manner so a third of the participants have shoe stickers, a third have cheek stickers, and a third have hand stickers.

Say: **Quickly form trios. Each trio needs one person with a shoe sticker, one person with a cheek sticker, and one person with a hand sticker.**

Give three blindfolds to each trio.

Say: **In your trios, tie the ankles of the person with the shoe sticker. Then blindfold the person with the cheek sticker. Finally, tie the wrists of the person with the hand sticker.**

When all the trios have completed this task, say: **Before class, I put a box of doughnuts in the church kitchen** (or any other place that's some distance from your room). **If you'd like to go help yourself to those doughnuts, you may. But you can't untie yourself or remove your blindfold. I think I'll go get a doughnut for myself.**

Leave the classroom without further comment. Technically, all of the participants can get to the doughnuts despite being tied or blindfolded—they can feel their way or hop. Supervise the participants to keep them from running into anything as you watch to see which trios cooperate and which try to go it alone. Then return to the classroom and take the doughnuts with you. Have participants remain tied or blindfolded as they enjoy their doughnuts and discuss these questions. Ask:

♦ **What went through your mind when I told you to help yourselves to the doughnuts in the kitchen?** (I was mad that my ankles were tied; I thought I'd never be able to get there; I wondered if I could find my way.)

♦ **How did you feel if your trio members left you behind?** (I worried that they wouldn't take care of me; I trusted them to bring me a doughnut.)

♦ **How did you respond when some trios started helping each other?** (I was glad I was part of a trio that worked together; I told my trio members that we should work together, too.)

♦ **What were the rewards for working together and taking care of one another?** (We all got doughnuts; I didn't have to feel guilty because I had a doughnut and no one else did.)

♦ **How was being blindfolded or having your feet or hands**

Teacher Tip

It's fine to have one or two groups of four. Encourage a good mix of ages in each group.

tied together like what happens to people in real life? (Some people have accidents or diseases that blind them or make it hard for them to get around.)

♦ **If you had to stay tied or blindfolded for a month, how would you want other people to treat you?** (I'd want to do most things for myself; I'd be glad to have other people help me.)

Say: **People have all kinds of difficulties in life— physical problems, losing a job or a home, failing at school— anything can happen. At times like that we need one another, just as you needed your trio members in this activity. ★ God wants us to be kind and loving. Let me introduce you to an old woman from the Bible whose life was turned around because someone was kind and loving to her.**

BIBLE STUDY

Tears to Laughter (Ruth 1–4)

You may want to have a woman from your congregation dress in a Bible-times costume and visit your class to present "Naomi's Story" on the next page. Or, quickly put on a costume and read the story yourself. Do it with a sparkle in your eye and a twist of Jewish humor. It's great fun for kids if a man presents the story in a falsetto voice.

Then lead participants in a round of applause for Naomi.

Have participants return to their trios to discuss the following questions. Pause after each question to allow for discussion.

♦ **What terrible things happened to Naomi?** (Her husband and sons died.)

♦ **How would you feel if you were the only one left in your family?** (Really sad; lonely.)

♦ **Why do you think Ruth went back to Bethlehem with Naomi?** (Because she felt sorry for Naomi; because she was a kind person.)

♦ **What good things happened because of Ruth's kindness?** (Ruth found a husband and had a baby; Naomi had a family again.)

♦ **When Ruth went with Naomi, do you think she expected any of these good things to happen? Why or why not?** (No, she only thought about helping her mother-in-law; she proba- bly trusted God to take care of her but didn't know about all the good things that would happen.)

Wave your hand to get everyone's attention, and then bring everyone together. Say: **★ God wants us to be kind and loving. Sometimes God gives us great surprises, like he did in today's story. But sometimes our reward is just the happiness we feel for having done something kind.**

NAOMI'S STORY

I've had a sad life, I tell you—a very sad life. But the living God has given me joy again! Do I look like a sad, old woman? Well, I'm not. I should say not! For God has filled my empty arms with a beautiful baby boy. A grandson! Can you believe it? A grandson born when my husband and sons were all in their graves. Let me tell you how it happened.

I grew up and married in the town of Bethlehem. When food was hard to find, my husband and my two sons and I moved to the land of Moab. Our sons married women from Moab, and for a time I was very happy.

But then my husband and sons died. I had no one left but my two daughters-in-law. I wailed and cried as they buried those men who were so dear to me. I felt empty. Empty and alone. So I decided to return to Bethlehem.

I told my two daughters-in-law to stay in Moab and find new husbands. One stayed behind. But Ruth insisted on going with me. "I'll go wherever you go," she said. "Your people will be my people, and your God will be my God."

You should've seen the looks on the faces of my old friends when we arrived back in Bethlehem. "Can it be Naomi?" they asked. I told them how empty and lonely I felt. No husband. No sons. Bah! What good is a lonely old woman?

But there was Ruth. Why should she stay with her old mother-in-law? She's one in a million, that girl.

It was harvest time, so Ruth went out into the fields to gather grain the workers left behind. The owner of the field was kind to her. "Come gather grain in my field every day," he said.

And who should that kind man be but Boaz—a close relative of mine. I knew Boaz would sleep by the piles of grain, to guard them. So I told Ruth to put on perfume and her best clothes and lie at the feet of Boaz. When Boaz awoke and found Ruth at his feet, Ruth said, "You are my relative. Will you take care of me?"

Ah, that Ruth. She's a lovely girl. Boaz decided to marry her and buy the land that belonged to my sons and my husband. That was nearly a year ago. And just last week, my grandson was born.

All my friends laughed and cried like a bunch of old hens. "Praise the Lord who gave you this grandson," they prayed. "May he become famous in Israel. He will give you new life and will take care of you in your old age because of your daughter-in-law who loves you. She is better for you than seven sons, because she has given birth to your grandson."

So who wouldn't be happy? Praise to the living God who fills me with joy!

LIFE APPLICATION

Love and Kindness to Go

Say: **Turn to your trio members once more. Take turns telling about a time when someone noticed that you were sad and did something kind to help or encourage you. Listen well, because in a moment you'll get to share what you heard from someone in your trio.**

Allow a couple of minutes for sharing. Then wave your hand to get everyone's attention and invite volunteers to share what they learned.

Say: **Now tell your trio members about someone you know who seems sad or discouraged, someone who could use some special love and kindness.**

Allow two or three minutes for sharing. Then wave your hand to get everyone's attention and say: **There are lots of ways to show love and kindness to people who are sad or discouraged—people in your own family, people at church, at school, or in your neighborhood. Let's have fun finding out how we can show love and kindness to all kinds of people.**

Choose one, two, or all three of these "Love and Kindness" learning-center ideas. Each is easy to prepare and fun for both kids and adults. (Consider photocopying the handouts on colored paper or stationery.)

♦ **Hearts-of-Kindness Coupon Center**—Participants make personalized kindness coupons to give away in decorated hearts. Set out photocopies of the "Hearts of Kindness" handout, scissors, tape, markers, and a finished sample.

♦ **Heart Pop-Up Card Center**—Participants make pop-up cards with encouraging messages to send to people who are sad. Set out photocopies of the "Someone Cares Pop-Up Card" handout, scissors, glue sticks, and a finished sample.

♦ **Love-and-Kindness Mix Center**—Set out bowls of cinnamon heart candies, small butter mints, and shredded coconut. You'll also need a small scoop for each bowl, sandwich bags, and ribbon. Photocopy the instructions found on the next page and set them out with the ingredients.

Love-and-Kindness Mix

Put a few cinnamon heart candies in a sandwich bag. Then add a scoop of small butter mints and a scoop of coconut. Tie the bag with a ribbon. Then give it to someone who would appreciate your gift of kindness!

Permission to photocopy this handout granted for local church use. Copyright © Lois Keffer. Published in *All-in-One Sunday School Volume 2* by Group Publishing, Inc., 1515 Cascade Ave., Loveland, CO 80538

Introduce the learning centers. Allow participants to choose where they'd like to begin. Encourage adults and older kids to work together with younger kids to help them complete their projects. If you have plenty of time, let participants do the projects at all three centers. Or, offer to send home photocopies of the handouts they didn't have time to complete.

As participants work, circulate among them and ask:

♦ **Who's the lucky person you're going to give this to?**

♦ **This looks great! Where are you going to mail it?**

♦ **Do you have plans for sharing this with someone?**

Announce when there are three minutes of working time left, then two minutes, then one. When you call time, have participants gather their projects and return to their trios.

COMMITMENT

Gift of Kindness

Say: **Show your trio members one thing you made. Then tell who you're going to give it to, and why you chose that person.**

Allow trios to share. Then wave your hand to get everyone's attention. Bring everyone together and ask:

♦ **How did you feel as you worked on projects that you knew would brighten someone's day?** (Warm and happy.)

Have a volunteer read Proverbs 14:21, 31.

♦ **Why is it important for Christians to be loving and kind?** (So we can show God's love; because we care about people; because it honors God.)

Say: ★ **God wants us to be loving and kind. The little gifts of kindness you've made today are just the beginning. God can show you many people who need your encouragement and love throughout the week.**

CLOSING

Blessing the Gifts

Ask everyone to hold a gift of kindness they made as you pray: **Lord, thank you for the beautiful story of Ruth and Naomi. We pray that you'll bless the gifts of kindness we made today. May they bring comfort and joy. We ask these things in Jesus' name, amen.**

HEARTS OF KINDNESS

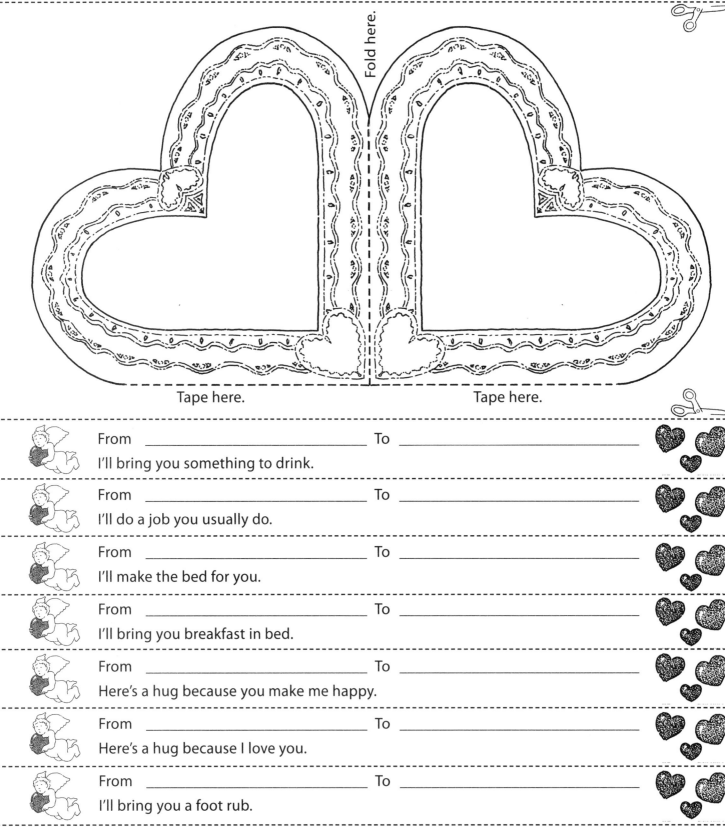

Fold here.

Tape here.

Tape here.

From _____ To _____
I'll bring you something to drink.

From _____ To _____
I'll do a job you usually do.

From _____ To _____
I'll make the bed for you.

From _____ To _____
I'll bring you breakfast in bed.

From _____ To _____
Here's a hug because you make me happy.

From _____ To _____
Here's a hug because I love you.

From _____ To _____
I'll bring you a foot rub.

Permission to photocopy this handout granted for local church use. Copyright © Lois Keffer.
Published in *All-in-One Sunday School Volume 2* by Group Publishing, Inc., 1515 Cascade Ave., Loveland, CO 80538.

SOMEONE CARES POP-UP CARD

1. Cut out the outside of the card.

2. Cut out the heart pop-up section and fold on the dotted lines.

3. Rub a glue stick on the back of the top and bottom hearts.

4. Place the point of the folded heart into the center of the fold of the card and press.

5. Voilà! When you open the card, the hearts pop up!

Fold on the dotted lines.

The Lord says, "I have loved you with an everlasting love; I have drawn you with loving-kindness" (from Jeremiah 31:3, NIV).

Cut heart outline.

Cut card outline.

Fold here.

SOMEONE CARES ABOUT YOU

Permission to photocopy this handout granted for local church use. Copyright © Lois Keffer.
Published in *All-in-One Sunday School Volume 2* by Group Publishing, Inc., 1515 Cascade Ave., Loveland, CO 80538.

LESSON AIM

To help kids understand that ★ God deserves first place in our lives.

OBJECTIVES

Kids will

✓ examine how they set priorities,
✓ learn why a rich young man chose not to follow Jesus,
✓ identify interests that may compete for first place in their lives, and
✓ make a commitment to put God first.

YOU'LL NEED

❑ 5 plates of treats*
❑ 5 paper grocery bags
❑ a "treasure box" (such as a jewelry box or tin canister)
❑ slips of paper
❑ a pencil
❑ Bibles
❑ photocopies of the "God Is First" handout (p. 122)
❑ scissors
❑ crayons or markers
❑ tape
Always check for allergies before serving snacks.

BIBLE BASIS

Mark 10:17-27

Many of Jesus' teachings challenge our minds and our sense of fairness as we attempt to understand them. The story of the rich young man is certainly one of those.

A sincere, respected young man comes to Jesus full of admiration and enthusiasm. He addresses Jesus as "good teacher," and

then goes straight to the heart of the matter: "What must I do to have life forever?"

Good start! Jesus' response is almost a retort: "Why do you call me good? Only God is good." Jesus isn't going to make this easy. Perhaps Jesus is warning the young man that flattery and emotion won't get what he's after. Jesus proceeds to name five of the commandments—those that deal with people-to-people relationships. You can almost see the light in the young man's eyes as he says, "I have obeyed all these things since I was a boy." Then Jesus lovingly issues the challenge: "Sell everything you have, and give the money to the poor. Then come and follow me."

The young man responds with stunned silence. Then he turns and sadly walks away, unable to part with his wealth and put God first in his life.

Matthew 6:33

Jesus challenges his followers to want God's will more than anything. Those who succeed in putting God first can trust God to take care of all the other things that so easily command their energy and attention.

Putting God first is a choice. It's never easy, but it's always the right choice—and the benefits are eternal.

UNDERSTANDING YOUR KIDS

Many things compete for first place in the lives of your kids. And those things may not be all bad! Older kids may be concerned about having top grades, being the best in sports or music, and identifying with the "in" group at school.

Younger kids may still be in the "me first" stage—what they want at the moment is most important; all other considerations are secondary.

Kids of all ages may be consumed with the desire to accumulate the most awesome collection of whatever toys or gizmos are the latest, greatest things to have.

Our challenge as Christian teachers is to show kids that God and God alone is worthy of our first loyalty. Good grades, medals, championships, and possessions may bring pleasure for a time. But in the eternal perspective, those things may become dangerous roadblocks preventing us from giving our very best to God.

This lesson will help kids evaluate their priorities and understand that ★ God deserves first place in our lives.

The Lesson 😊

ATTENTION GRABBER

What's First?

Before kids arrive, set out five plates of special things such as quarters, strawberries, chocolate kisses, gummy worms, and gum. Cover the plates with paper grocery bags and don't let anyone peek! Plan to have at least two treats for each child.

Tell kids they'll choose from the items on the plates, but they have to wait their turn. Line kids from youngest to the oldest. Remove the bags and let kids see what's on the plates.

Say to the first child in line: **Go the table and take one thing. Then go to the back of the line.**

Explain that kids can choose one thing each time they're at the front of the line. Encourage kids to eat their treat if they've chosen something edible. Keep going until everyone has chosen two treats. Then gather kids in a circle and ask:

♦ **How did you decide what to take first?** (I took what I like best; I took a quarter because I can buy something with it later; I took gummy worms because they're gross.)

♦ **What was easy about deciding what to take? What was difficult about deciding?** (It was easy because I really love strawberries; it was hard because I like everything.)

♦ **Would you agree that all these treats are good things? Then why are there still things left on some of the plates?** (Because you said we could only take two things; because the things that are all gone were better than the things that are left.)

Say: **Sometimes it's hard to decide between what's good and what's best. Even though you like the things up here, you had only two choices. You had to decide what to take first, what to take second, and what not to take. We have to make choices about what comes first in life, too. Today we're going to learn that ★ God deserves first place in our lives.**

BIBLE STUDY

A Rich Young Man (Mark 10:17-27)

Say: **Our Bible story today is about a rich young man. Let's see what it'd be like to be rich.** Show your "treasure box." Choose a child who's a quick writer to be your scribe. Give your scribe a pencil and several slips of paper. Choose a younger child to hold the box and put the paper in it.

Say: **Let's name things a rich person today has. Our scribe will note them; then we'll put them in our treasure box.**

Children may name things such as wealth, a big house, cars, a swimming pool, and fancy clothes. When children have contributed several ideas, pick up the treasure box and hug it. Ask:

♦ **How would you feel if you had all this?** (Good; happy.)

♦ **What would you do if someone told you to give all these things away?** (I'd laugh; I'd say no; I'd ask why.)

Say: **Let's see what happened to the rich young man.**

Choose two good readers, one for the rich young man's words, and one for Jesus' words. Open your Bibles to Mark 10:17. Explain that you'll be the narrator. Cue your readers with a nod when it's time for them to read. Close the reading at the end of verse 27. Then ask:

♦ **What did Jesus ask the young man to do?** (Sell everything; give money to the poor and follow him.)

♦ **Why do you think the young man went away sad?** (Because he was rich and didn't want to sell everything.)

♦ **What do you think was most important to the young man?** (Keeping his riches.)

♦ **Do you think the young man cared about Jesus? Explain.** (Yes, because he came to Jesus and asked what to do; no, because he wouldn't do what Jesus asked.)

♦ **How do you think Jesus felt when the young man walked away?** (Sad; disappointed.)

Say: **The Bible tells us that ★ God deserves first place in our lives. Jesus must have been sad when the young man decided that his riches were more important than obeying and following Jesus. It's not always easy for us to put God first in our lives, either.**

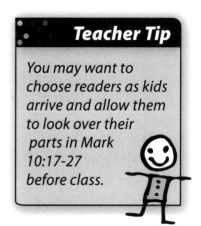

Teacher Tip

You may want to choose readers as kids arrive and allow them to look over their parts in Mark 10:17-27 before class.

LIFE APPLICATION

God Is First

Say: **Let's have some fun thinking about things we enjoy—things that are important to us.**

Distribute photocopies of the "God Is First" handout, scissors, and markers or crayons. Form groups of four. Make sure there's at least one reader in each group who can help nonreaders understand how to complete the handout. Circulate among the groups and offer help to any who need it.

Have kids cut out the completed quilt squares and share what they wrote or drew with the other members of their groups. Then gather everyone together and ask:

♦ **What new things did you learn about the people in your group?** (Stacey does gymnastics; Jon likes to read.)

Say: **It looks like we have some really interesting people in this class! I'm glad to see that you're involved in so many wonderful things.**

COMMITMENT

Hidden Cross

Say: **Let's take a moment to read the Bible verse that's printed in the center of your handout.**

Have a volunteer read Matthew 6:33 aloud. Then ask:

♦ **What does this verse tell you about the things you wrote or drew?** (That they're not as important as God; that those things are good, but God should be #1 in our lives.)

♦ **What happens when something becomes more important than God?** (We get in trouble; it makes God sad.)

♦ **What do you see in this design besides triangles and squares?** Encourage kids to study the handout until someone realizes that the design makes a cross.

Say: ★ **God deserves first place in our lives. When we make loving and obeying God the most important thing we do, our lives are like a beautiful pattern, with God in the center.**

Have kids re-form their groups and discuss this question:

♦ **What does putting God first mean to you?** (Taking time to learn about God; praying every day; obeying what the Bible says.)

Challenge kids to sign their names in the center square to show their commitment to give God first place in their lives.

Say: **Now tell the members of your group one thing you'll do to give God first place in your life this week.**

After groups have shared, call kids together and encourage them to share what they learned in their group discussions.

CLOSING

Off the Wall

Invite one group of four to tape its squares together on a wall, as shown in the illustration. Then invite the other groups to add their squares. Help kids arrange their squares so the completed display forms a connected design. Ask:

♦ **What does our display make you think of?** (A pretty quilt; that God puts us all together like this in our church; that we make a beautiful pattern together.) Hold up the treasure box.

Say: **The rich young man had many beautiful things in his life. But because those things were more important to him than God, he went away sad.** Gesture toward the wall display. **We have wonderful things in our lives, too. But ★ God deserves first place in our lives. Jesus said that when we give God first place, God will take care of everything else.**

Close class with a prayer similar to this one: **Lord, thank you for loving us and filling our lives with wonderful things. Please help us give you first place in our lives, and we'll trust you to take care of everything else. In Jesus' name, amen.**

Teacher Tip

If your kids enjoy art, encourage them to color in the small triangles. Consider preparing a colored sample before class to help kids visualize how the finished square might look. When the colored squares are assembled on the wall during the closing activity, they'll make a beautiful display.

GOD IS FIRST

What things are important to you? Write or draw the people, place, hobby, and interest that are most important to you in the four corners of the square below. You may want to color in all the small triangles. Then cut out the completed square.

Important people

Important place

"But seek first [God's] kingdom and his righteousness, and all these things will be given to you as well" (Matthew 6:33, NIV).

_____ puts God first.

Important hobby

Special interest

Permission to photocopy this handout granted for local church use. Copyright © Lois Keffer.
Published in *All-in-One Sunday School Volume 2* by Group Publishing, Inc., 1515 Cascade Ave., Loveland, CO 80538.

LESSON AIM

To help kids learn that ★ Jesus is with us in tough times.

Teacher Tip

This lesson works well with an intergenerational class. You may wish to invite whole families to join you for this session.

OBJECTIVES

Kids will

✓ play a game involving safety zones,
✓ learn how Jesus took care of the disciples' fears,
✓ identify times when they're afraid, and
✓ trust God to help them deal with their fears.

YOU'LL NEED

❑ masking tape or rope
❑ a roll of dimes
❑ a cuddly stuffed animal
❑ photocopies of the "Jesus Is My Safety Zone" handout (p. 130)
❑ pencils

BIBLE BASIS

Matthew 8:23-27

The Sea of Galilee was notorious for its sudden storms. The disciples, though some of them were experienced fishermen who had literally spent a lifetime on that body of water, were terrified when their little craft began to toss helplessly on the crashing waves in the middle of the night. They were amazed—and frustrated—that Jesus lay calmly sleeping in the front of the boat. Wasn't he aware of their peril? Didn't he care?

Jesus used the opportunity to demonstrate he is truly master of the wind and the waves. Jesus is master of the storms that buffet our lives, as well. Sometimes we may be tempted to wonder, as the disciples did, if he knows what's happening in our lives or if he cares. What we learn from this story is Jesus may not always make the storms disappear immediately, but he will walk with us through them.

Matthew 28:20

Jesus is the friend who sticks closer than a brother. Though kids may legitimately long for the reassuring physical presence of a trusted adult, Jesus' promise to be with those who trust in him is powerful indeed.

UNDERSTANDING YOUR KIDS

"What's there to be afraid of?" I can remember my father asking that question when I was just a wee tot and the night-frights kept me from falling asleep. What's there to be afraid of? Plenty! Shadowy corners, familiar objects that loomed huge and strange in the dark, unknown things under the bed and behind the closet door, and the something that might pop up to get you if you got up to go to the bathroom. You may smile at that list, but children's fears are very real to them, and wise adults will take those fears seriously.

Kids of this generation have a lot more to handle than that standard list of fears. One of kids' biggest anxieties is being separated from parents. Divorce rates give credibility to that fear. On top of that, the television imports all kinds of fears right into living rooms—everything from war to psychopathic killers.

Now more than ever, kids of all ages need the assurance that God can be a personal, comforting, protecting presence in their lives.

The Lesson 😊

Teacher Tip

Adjust the rules of this game to work for your group. You can make the boundaries of the game as large or as small as space permits. If too many people succeed in getting to the corners and back, let two or three people be "It." To even the odds for younger kids, let three of them be It at the same time.

ATTENTION GRABBER

Safety Zone

Set up the play area for this game by establishing four corners and a center circle as safety zones. Mark off the center circle with masking tape or rope; make it large enough so everyone can stand in it comfortably. Mark off a small triangle at each corner. Kids who are inside the circle and the corner triangles will be safe. Choose one person to be "It."

If you have adults in your class today, have them form the safety zones. Assign one adult to each corner and have the rest outline the center circle.

Say: **You can score a point and win a dime each time you run from the circle to one of the corners and back to the circle without being tagged. The circle and the corners are safety zones—you can't be tagged there. But only one person at a time can be in each corner. If you get tagged, you're frozen until another player tags you to unfreeze you.**

Stand in the center circle to hand out dimes as players score. Also be prepared to act as referee to determine whether or not kids make it to the safety zones before they're tagged.

Have a new person be It each time five people have scored.

Stop the game before interest lags. Bring kids together and help them focus on what you're about to say by leading them in some deep breaths.

Ask:

♦ **How did it feel to leave the safety zone?** (Scary; exciting.)

♦ **How did it feel to score and win a dime?** (It felt good; I wanted to win more.)

♦ **Which did you want to do more—stay safe or score? Explain.** (I wanted to score; I was afraid to try, I just wanted to stay safe.)

♦ **This game had safety zones where nothing bad could happen to you; do you have safety zones in real life? What are they?** (Home and church are my safety zones; my safety zone is when I'm with my parents or good friends because I know they won't let anything bad happen to me.)

♦ **How does it feel to go outside those safety zones?** (Really scary; it doesn't really bother me; I like to be out on my own.)

♦ **Why do you think people sometimes leave their safety zones even if they don't want to?** (Sometimes people have to move to a new place; sometimes parents divorce and we lose part of our safety zone; accidents and sickness sometimes pull us away from our safety zones.)

Say: It's wonderful to have places where we feel safe and people who we feel safe with. But we can't always stay in our safety zones. And even in our safety zones scary things can sometimes happen. That's when it's nice to know Jesus is at our side. ★ Jesus is with us in tough times.

BIBLE STUDY

Calming the Storm (Matthew 8:23-27)

Say: **Today we're going to listen to a really scary story about what happened to Jesus' disciples. And you're going to help me tell it.**

Practice each of these cues and responses with the class:

♦ Whenever I say "boat," everyone say "creeeak" and pretend you're pulling hard on the oars.

♦ Whenever I say "disciples," all the boys (and men) count to 12 really fast.

♦ Whenever I say "wind," the girls (and women) cup their hands around their mouths and blow.

♦ Whenever I say "waves," put your hands side by side and make waves in front of you.

♦ Whenever I say "Jesus," point to upward and say, "Christ, the Lord."

As you tell the "Jesus Calms the Sea" story on the next page, be sure to put an emphasis on each of the underlined words; then pause for kids to respond.

Say: **Here we go! Everybody stick together so you don't get too scared.**

Read the story. After you finish, have kids give themselves a round of applause for helping you tell the story. Then ask:

♦ **What happened that made the disciples feel unsafe?** (Their boat got in a bad storm; they were afraid of drowning.)

♦ **What did they do to get help?** (They woke Jesus up.)

♦ **What did Jesus do to make things okay again?** (He told the wind and the waves to be still.)

♦ **How could he do that?** (He's God's son—he can do anything.)

♦ **Can Jesus help us the way he helped the disciples in the storm? Why or why not?** (Yes, Jesus can still do anything; no, he doesn't work that way now.)

♦ **Can Jesus help us even though we can't see him or touch him? Why or why not?** (Yes, he's always with us; no, sometimes we don't ask him.)

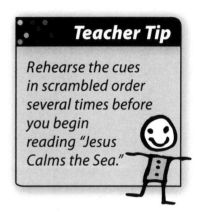

Teacher Tip

Rehearse the cues in scrambled order several times before you begin reading "Jesus Calms the Sea."

LIFE APPLICATION

Someone to Hang On To

Ask:

♦ **Can anybody tell how Jesus helped you in a scary situation?** Give kids a chance to share. It would be helpful to share a story from your own experience too. If you have other adults in the class, they might also tell a story, too.

After people have shared, bring out a cuddly stuffed animal. Pass it around and have everyone hug it. In a larger class pass two or three stuffed animals at once. Ask:

♦ **Why do you think people like to have stuffed animals around?** (They're cute; they feel good to hold.)

♦ **How do you feel when you hug an animal like this?** (It feels warm; cuddly; good.)

♦ **Do you ever hug a stuffed animal when you're scared or sad?** (Sometimes.)

♦ **How is the feeling you get from hugging a stuffed animal like how it feels to trust Jesus when you're scared or sad?** (Jesus comforts me; I remember he loves me.)

♦ **How is trusting Jesus different from hugging a stuffed animal?** (Jesus is really alive and has power to help me.)

COMMITMENT

Facing Our Fears

Say: **Just before Jesus went back to heaven, he made a promise to his followers. Let's look at that promise.**

Give each person a copy of the "Jesus Is My Safety Zone" handout and a pencil. Point out the Bible verse at the bottom.

Say: **This is the promise I'm talking about. Let's read it together.**

Say: **This is what I really want you to remember from today's class. Jesus promises he will always be with us. And having Jesus with us is even better than having a teddy bear or an older brother, or even parents, because Jesus is the Son of God, and he has power to help us!** ★ **Jesus is with us in tough times.**

Have kids (and adults) use the space on the handout to draw or write about a scary situation they sometimes face. Allow two or three minutes for drawing and writing, and then ask volunteers each to tell about the scary situations they put on their handout. Kids may be surprised to learn adults have fears, too, and even though they're grown up, they also trust in Jesus to help them in scary situations.

Ask:

♦ **How does it feel to see Jesus with his arms around you in**

Teacher Tip

If you have a very large inter-generational class, you may wish to form two or three groups. Encourage people in each group to share how God helped them through scary situations.

Teacher Tip

Younger children will be able to "read" the verse after the class repeats it a couple of times.

JESUS CALMS THE SEA

The disciples were just exhausted. All day crowds and crowds of people had been following Jesus, listening as he taught and watching as he healed the sick. Now the sun was beginning to set over the Sea of Galilee. Seeing how tired his disciples were, Jesus said, "Let's get in a boat and go over to the other side of the lake." It would be good for all of them to get away from the crowds for a while.

The disciples rowed away from the shore while Jesus went to the front of the boat and lay down on a cushion. The waves lapped gently against the side of the boat, lulling Jesus into a peaceful sleep.

But suddenly a wind began to blow dark clouds across the sky. The waves weren't so gentle anymore. The little boat began to pitch and rock. The disciples began to get a little worried. But Jesus still lay sleeping in the front of the boat.

Then the wind grew stronger still. The spray from the waves got the disciples all wet. This was getting to be a bad storm! But Jesus still lay sleeping in the front of the boat.

By the time the fishing boat reached the center of the lake, the wind had turned into a angry gale that whipped the waves so high they washed right over the boat. The disciples were terrified. They thought they might drown. But Jesus still lay sleeping in the front of the boat.

Finally, someone went and shook Jesus. "Master," he cried, "don't you care if we drown?" Jesus looked around. He listened to the howling wind. He felt the cold, stinging spray as waves crashed over the little boat. He saw the fear in the faces of his disciples. Then Jesus stood, stretched out his arms to the wind and the waves, and commanded: "Peace! Be still!" And all at once the wind died down and the waves became completely calm. Then he asked the disciples: "Why are you so afraid? Where is your faith?"

Jesus showed his power over the wind and the waves that day on the Sea of Galilee. Just as he cared for his disciples in that little storm-tossed boat, he will care for you.

your scary situation? (It feels good.)

Say: **The next time you're afraid, I hope you'll remember**
★ **Jesus is with us in tough times.**

CLOSING

Always There

Gather everyone in the Safety Zone circle. If you have adults in the class, have them make an outer circle with the kids inside.

Close with a prayer similar to this one: **Jesus, thank you for being our safety zone. Help us to remember the next time we're really scared that you are with us. Amen.**

Draw or write about a scary situation that worries you. Then remember Jesus' promise to be with you!

JESUS IS MY SAFETY ZONE

"Teach these new disciples to obey all the commands I have taught you. And be sure of this: I am with you always, even to the end of the age" Matthew 28:20.

Permission to photocopy this handout granted for local church use. Copyright © Lois Keffer.
Published in *All-in-One Sunday School Volume 2* by Group Publishing, Inc., 1515 Cascade Ave., Loveland, CO 80538.